OVER THE MOON

A Magical and Hilarious Pantomime

Michael Buchanan-Smart

Jasper Publishing

1 Broad St Hemel Hempstead Herts HP2 5BW
Tel; 01442 63461 Fax; 01442 217102

Jasper Publishing

1 Broad Street Hemel Hempstead
Herts HP2 5BW
Tel; 01442 63461 Fax; 01442 217102

ISBN 1 874009 61 9

CHARACTERS

Man in the Moon

Prince Lionheart	
Dame Laughalot	His Nanny
Rainbow	The Palace Magician
Snowflake	A Princess
Icicle	Her friend
Ice Queen	
Jack Frost	Her protégé
Lottery	Prince's Lucky Messenger
Tollkeeper/Rainmaker/	
Gardener/Jack Pot	

Rudolph	The Cow
Prudence	The Cat
Smelly	The Dog
Trumper	A Village Dog
Dish and Spoon	

Plus Various Small Parts in some routines

General Chorus and dancers as: Courtiers, Villagers, Frosties, Snowflakes, Mibbie Mibbies, Sunrays, Raindrops, Rainbow Colours etc.,

SYNOPSIS OF SCENES

The two main scenes are 'The Palace Grounds' and 'Buttercup Meadow' and you may wish to construct sets for these. The two minor scenes are 'Black Forest Pathway' and 'Village at Murky Marshlands'. These scenes may perhaps be placed on the back of the main scenes. See 'Stage' notes on page 64 for detailed hints on stage construction.

NOTES ON THE CHARACTERS

Man in the Moon. The 'heart' of the panto. Must be a boisterous, robust character. Jolly with a delicate sense of humour. Wise and just. He is saddened, and wants to be happy again, and the romantic force of old. On stage nearly all the time, in his moon. Male, preferably middle-aged or older, with a sound voice.

Dame Laughalot. A lovable 'silly' character, who laughs at everything, even her own misfortunes. Blustery, flippity, and will do anything to help her Prince. Carries the main laughter situations. Initially under the spell of the Palace Magician, but finally finds true love elsewhere. Male, any age.

Prince Lionheart. A happy, dashing, brave and forthright Prince. Sad when he almost loses his Kingdom and Snowflake, but primarily a confident, glamorous 'swashbuckling' hero, equal to the challenges presented. He gains wisdom from the Man in the Moon. Principal boy, therefore female.

Snowflake. Principal girl. Pretty, petite, delicate and feminine. Falls in love with the Prince. Daughter of the wicked Ice Queen, but confident that the Prince will find a way to make their love last for ever. Female.

Rainbow. The Palace Magician. Likeable and lovable. His tricks invariably go wrong. A colourful character, to match his costume. A personality part. Preferably male.

Lottery. The lucky messenger of the Prince, speaking in rhymed couplets and using wide sweeping gestures. A dry sense of humour with both good news and bad news. Can be played campish to good effect. Male or female.

Ice Queen. A sleek, cold and calculating ruler of the ice regions, determined to freeze the world. Haughty and arrogant, hating the Man in the Moon. Her wickedness knows no bounds. Female, any age.

Jack Frost. Mischievous and cheeky character who does the Ice Queen's bidding. Not really wicked, but can be quite cunning. A bit of a rascal. Falls in love with Icicle, at the end, and 'melts' away with her. Male or female.

Icicle. Easy going - here today and gone tomorrow. Caught up in her cold world, but a friendly soul. Very 'Hip' and perhaps 'jazzy'. A 'cool' character. Helps Snowflake as much as she can, and falls for the charms of Jack Frost. Female.

Tollkeeper. Who becomes in turn; a Rainmaker, a Gardener and Jack Pot. As Tollkeeper a money grabbing official, as Rainmaker a cantankerous, comical type, as Gardener a country bumpkin. Wins the lottery, and the Dame! A demanding part. Male or female any age.

Rudolph. Suggest a one-person cow. A little dithery, but can be quite abrupt. Has a bright red nose. Male or female.

Prudence. Soft and fluffy. Feline and comfort loving. Female juvenile.

Smelly. A snappy dog, who likes fun. Sniffs and laughs a lot, and takes a fancy to Trumper. Male juvenile.

Trumper. Fluffy female dog, who can be quite naughty. Female juvenile.

Courtier/Villagers. Generally friendly and jolly, though saddened and angry at times. Becoming more jovial and courageous as they sense the growing optimism of the Prince. They want the Ice Queen destroyed.

Juveniles. Involved as Courtiers and Villagers, and also playing the parts of;

> **Frosties.** Mischievous underlings of Jack Frost who spread the cold of the night.
>
> **Mibbie Mibbies.** Forest imps who inhabit the Black Forest. They are quick and 'nip' and 'bite' their prey, and like a bit of fun.
>
> **Sunrays/Raindrops/Snowflakes.** The first two are appropriately named, and mingle together to create the rainbow. Snowflakes flutter around Snowflake.
>
> **Rainbow Colours.** Seven or fourteen juveniles who perform the 'Rainbow Dance'. (see Costume and Stage notes)
>
> **Dish and Spoon.** Can be one juvenile performer (dish carrying a spoon) or two performers.

There are possibilities for the juvenile roles here to be doubled up, depending on how many you have available.

MUSICAL NUMBERS

The songs included here are suggestions only for the type of music that can be used. Final choice is left to the Musical Director.

Please note that permission from **Jasper Publishing** to perform this play **does not** include permission to use copyright songs and music suggested here. Performers are urged to consult the **Performing Right Society** (see note below).

1.	**Page 2** 'Happiness' or 'I See The Moon, The Moon Sees Me'	Full chorus
2.	**Page 7** 'I Wanna Be Rainbow's (Bobby's) Girl'	Dame and juveniles
3.	**Page 12** 'I'm H. A. P. P. Y. I'm H. A. P. P. Y.'	Dame
4.	**Page 13** 'Blue Moon' or 'Moonlight Becomes You'	Prince and Snowflake
5.	**Page 16** 'Here We Go, Here We Go' or 'Walk On'	Prince, Dame, Lottery, Rainbow, and chorus
6.	**Page 16** 'I Know A Song That'll Get On Your Nerves'	PrinceDame Rainbow, Lottery
7.	**Page 19** 'Ging Gang Gooley Gooley'	Prince, Dame, Rainbow, Lottery
8.	**Page 22** 'By The Light Of The Silvery Moon'	Jack Frost, Icicle and juveniles
9.	**Page 29** 'My Favourite Things'	Dame
10.	**Page 29** 'Sun Arise, Bring In De Morning'	Dame
11.	**Page 30** 'Always Look On The Bright Side Of Life' or 'Happy Wanderer'	Prince, Dame, Rainbow, Lottery and chorus
12.	**Page 31** 'Oh What A Beautiful Morning'	Full chorus
13.	**Page 33** 'One Man Went To Mow'	Villager
14.	**Page 36** 'Bring Me Sunshine'	Rainmaker
15.	**Page 37** 'Sing A Rainbow'	Full chorus and juvenile dance
16.	**Page 42** 'Magic Moments' or 'Love Changes Everything'	Prince, Snowflake
17.	**Page 46** 'Here We Go (are) Again'	Full chorus
18.	**Page 48** 'Come And Drink Ale (wine) With Me'	Tollkeeper, Dame
19.	**Page 50** 'I Can See Clearly Now The Snow (rain) Has Gone'	Prince and chorus
20.	**Page 54** 'I'm Gonna Marry You-Oo' or 'My Friend The Moon Man'	Prince, Dame, Jack Frost and chorus

Author's Note

To me the Moon is timeless, and as such is worthy of a modern day pantomime. Whilst researching I came across two oddities that may be of interest. First is that in 1826 a pantomime was written, 'The Man in the Moon', and was related in some way to the Battle of Waterloo. *(I am at a loss to expand on this)* Perhaps more of note is that 'The Emperor of the Moon' was apparently the real starting influence of pantomimes in England. It was written by Aphra Behn (1640-89) an English novelist and playright, and it was he who re-introduced speech to 'Harlequin' who had, for the previous century, only mimed.

Acknowledgements

I would like to say a special thank you to Howard and Mark Southgate for writing the music to *'Over The Moon Of Love'*, as I envisaged it, but far better.

Also thank you to Brian Corrie for the design of a splendid front cover.

I would like to mention PADS (Peverel Amateur Dramatic Society) President Dorothy Shands. It was an inspiration working with the group on this the first of (hopefully) my many pantomimes. Thank you Dorothy, and all you fellow 'Thespians'.

Last, but not least, I would like to dedicate **Over The Moon** to my wife Ella, for her belief in me, and for her help, support and understanding during its creation.

MUSICAL NUMBERS

The songs included here are suggestions only for the type of music that can be used. Final choice is left to the Musical Director.

Please note that permission from **Jasper Publishing** to perform this play **does not** include permission to use copyright songs and music suggested here. Performers are urged to consult the **Performing Right Society** (see note below).

1.	**Page 2** 'Happiness' or 'I See The Moon, The Moon Sees Me'	Full chorus
2.	**Page 7** 'I Wanna Be Rainbow's (Bobby's) Girl'	Dame and juveniles
3.	**Page 12** 'I'm H. A. P. P. Y. I'm H. A. P. P. Y.'	Dame
4.	**Page 13** 'Blue Moon' or 'Moonlight Becomes You'	Prince and Snowflake
5.	**Page 16** 'Here We Go, Here We Go' or 'Walk On'	Prince, Dame, Lottery, Rainbow, and chorus
6.	**Page 16** 'I Know A Song That'll Get On Your Nerves'	PrinceDame Rainbow, Lottery
7.	**Page 19** 'Ging Gang Gooley Gooley'	Prince, Dame, Rainbow, Lottery
8.	**Page 22** 'By The Light Of The Silvery Moon'	Jack Frost, Icicle and juveniles
9.	**Page 29** 'My Favourite Things'	Dame
10.	**Page 29** 'Sun Arise, Bring In De Morning'	Dame
11.	**Page 30** 'Always Look On The Bright Side Of Life' or 'Happy Wanderer'	Prince, Dame, Rainbow, Lottery and chorus
12.	**Page 31** 'Oh What A Beautiful Morning'	Full chorus
13.	**Page 33** 'One Man Went To Mow'	Villager
14.	**Page 36** 'Bring Me Sunshine'	Rainmaker
15.	**Page 37** 'Sing A Rainbow'	Full chorus and juvenile dance
16.	**Page 42** 'Magic Moments' or 'Love Changes Everything'	Prince, Snowflake
17.	**Page 46** 'Here We Go (are) Again'	Full chorus
18.	**Page 48** 'Come And Drink Ale (wine) With Me'	Tollkeeper, Dame
19.	**Page 50** 'I Can See Clearly Now The Snow (rain) Has Gone'	Prince and chorus
20.	**Page 54** 'I'm Gonna Marry You-Oo' or 'My Friend The Moon Man'	Prince, Dame, Jack Frost and chorus

Song No 21 'Over The Moon Of Love' has been specially written for this pantomime, and should be used. Copies of the sheet music are available from **Jasper Publishing**.

Songs suggested here are considered to be popular songs, and although some may be quite old, they are still very 'catchy', and should be popular with parents and children. Make changes according to local mood, technical ability of cast and musicians etc.,

A pantomime should be brisk, and very often a song is too long to keep the pace going. Reduce any song as necessary, to keep within two to two and a half minutes, maximum. Length of comedy songs depend on the reaction, or involvement, of audience. Decide the length at the outset, or play by ear.

*The following statement (provided by the **Performing Right Society Ltd.,**) concerning the use of music, is included here for your attention.*

The permission of the owner of the performing right in copyright music must be obtained before any public performance may be given, whether in conjunction with a play or sketch or otherwise, and this permission is just as necessary for amateur performances as for professional. The majority of copyright musical works (other than oratorios, musical plays and similar dramatico-musical works) are controlled in the British Commonwealth by the **Performing Right Society Ltd., 29-33 Berners Street, London W1P 4AA.**

The Society's practice is to issue licences authorising the use of its repertoire to the proprietors of premises at which music is publicly performed, or, alternatively, to the organisers of musical entertainment, but the Society does not require payment of fees by performers as such. Producers or promoters of plays, sketches etc., at which music is to be performed, during or after the play or sketch, should ascertain whether the premises at which the performances are to be given are covered by a licence issued by the Society, and if they are not, should make application to the Society for particulars as to the fee payable.

Promoting and Advertising

This pantomime is based around the nursery rhyme:

> Hey diddle diddle, the Cat and the Fiddle,
> The Cow jumped over the Moon,
> The Little Dog laughed to see such fun,
> And the Dish ran away with the Spoon.

When promoting 'Over the Moon', or for additions to your posters and programmes etc., it is suggested that some or all of the following are used together with normal standards of; Traditional, Magical, Hilarious etc.,

* * * * * * * * * *

Hilarious as the Cow (Rudolph) tries to jump over the Moon and lands on the Dame, and Dog (Smelly) chases the Dish and Spoon through audience.

Be amazed as, at the speed of light, the Man in the Moon makes 'Time Stand Still' to find the special secret.

Marvel at the magic of Rainbow, the Colourful Magician, with his little 'Wobbly Wand'.

Laugh at the waving antics of Lottery, the rhyming Lucky Messenger, and when the Prince and his friends are attacked by the nipping and biting Mibbie Mibbies in the Forest.

Boo the wicked Ice Queen as with her accomplices Jack Frost and his 'jazzy' girlfriend Icicle she attempts to freeze the Prince's Palace and Kingdom, attacking with Frosties and Mibbie Mibbies through the audience.

Crazy comedy as the Dame (out of her trolley) escapes her 'sell by date' and finds happiness with Jack Pot.

Spectacular 'Rainbow Dance' of Sunrays and Raindrops.

True romance as Prince Lionheart and Snowflake (and other happy couples) sing 'Over The Moon Of Love', followed by a real confetti wedding.

For all the family - lively songs, action and comedy in which the children and adults can join in the fun.

These phrases do not give away the plot, but represent some of the important aspects and routines.

Author's Note

To me the Moon is timeless, and as such is worthy of a modern day pantomime. Whilst researching I came across two oddities that may be of interest. First is that in 1826 a pantomime was written, 'The Man in the Moon', and was related in some way to the Battle of Waterloo. *(I am at a loss to expand on this)* Perhaps more of note is that 'The Emperor of the Moon' was apparently the real starting influence of pantomimes in England. It was written by Aphra Behn (1640-89) an English novelist and playright, and it was he who re-introduced speech to 'Harlequin' who had, for the previous century, only mimed.

Acknowledgements

I would like to say a special thank you to Howard and Mark Southgate for writing the music to *'Over The Moon Of Love'*, as I envisaged it, but far better.

Also thank you to Brian Corrie for the design of a splendid front cover.

I would like to mention PADS (Peverel Amateur Dramatic Society) President Dorothy Shands. It was an inspiration working with the group on this the first of (hopefully) my many pantomimes. Thank you Dorothy, and all you fellow 'Thespians'.

Last, but not least, I would like to dedicate **Over The Moon** to my wife Ella, for her belief in me, and for her help, support and understanding during its creation.

OVER THE MOON

PROLOGUE

Whilst the audience are taking their seats, it is suggested that 'Moonlight Sonata' is played as background music, and when all are seated, the Prologue is spoken. A Spokesperson from the Theatre Club, speaking prior to the curtains opening on the First Act

Spokesperson Ladies and gentlemen, and most important of all, children - welcome. How wonderful of you to be here this evening (afternoon) when you could all have stayed at home in the warm, watching television. What you are about to see is a tale of love over hate, happiness and laughter over misery, and above all, good over evil.

The Man in the Moon is losing his powers of warmth, magic and romance as the wicked Ice Queen transforms all the lands to a cold and shivering landscape. But all is not lost, as the Man in the Moon guides the Prince of the Kingdom, and his loyal friends, on a journey to the 'End of the Rainbow' to seek the secret of how to stop the Ice Queen.

Whilst all around him is beginning to freeze, the Prince meets, and falls in love with Snowflake, a snow maiden, but if the Ice Queen succeeds with her plans, will the Prince and Snowflake ever be together? What can he do? Will the battle with the Ice Queen be won? Will the power and happiness of the Man in the Moon be restored? And will goodness triumph and prevail over wickedness? Let us wait and see for ourselves.

Pray join me now for a truly wonderful and spectacular tale of excitement, laughter, magic and romance, and for the next two hours the adults too can be children.

I give you - Over the Moon!

ACT 1

Scene 1

The Palace Grounds at Sunset. The Courtyard of a Medieval Castle with battlements in the background. On stage right is a 'false turret' over which a large moon is shining, in which the Man in the Moon is sleeping. The courtiers are quite grandly dressed. They dance a sort of stepping motion to the side/ front, and some 'under/overs' can be included. Do a twirl at the end of each chorus line of 'Happiness'; as the song ends (on a high note) all to the front of stage with arms raised/wide. Make it full of zest to get a good start to the pantomime

Song No 1

Chorus sing, 'Happiness' or 'I See The Moon, The Moon Sees Me'. As the music and dance end, the Man in the Moon sits up in his moon, stretching and yawning

Man in Moon Lords, ladies and gentlefolk, I know I was already awakening and you are without doubt a wonderful alarm, but gently please, I have little enough sleep with these long winter nights.

Courtier 1 We have been so happy lately, we wanted to share our happiness with you.

Courtier 2 We didn't really want to wake you, you looked so tranquil, so peaceful.

Courtier 3 But we are glad you are now awake, Man in the Moon, for we need your help to stop us being frozen by the wicked Ice Queen.

Courtier 5 We hear that she intends to freeze all the lands, and take away the warmth, love and romance from our lives.

Courtiers *(all)* Yes! Yes! Please help us! We don't want to be cold! Don't let our children freeze etc.,

Man in Moon Wait! Wait a moment! Listen to me please. On my travels last night, I saw that the Ice Queen has frozen the continents to the east and west of the oceans. *(looking out)* And you are right, all is not well here. I can see now that the lands in the north are all covered with snow, and I fear that the ice is creeping nearer to you.

Courtier 1 Please help us Man in the Moon - save us from the wicked Ice Queen.

Man in Moon I will try, but I sense the Ice Queen's forces are too strong and reach beyond our lands. I too am feeling the cold and my powers are beginning to wane, as is my happiness, to see such misery and coldness on your earth.

Courtier 2 What can we do? Is there no hope?

Courtier 3 Please Man in the Moon, you must help us destroy the evil Ice Queen.

Man in Moon There is a way. You must discover the secret that is hidden at the 'End of the Rainbow' it will help you to stop the Ice Queen.

Courtier 4 How can we reach the end of the rainbow? It always moves away. It cannot be reached.

Man in Moon The end of the rainbow can be reached, but the secret can only
   be revealed to a person of Royal blood.

Courtier 5 The Prince!

Courtier 1 Yes, the Prince. He will find the secret of how to destroy the evil Ice
   Queen.

Courtier 2 He must, before we are frozen to death.

Courtier 3 Where is the Prince?

Courtier 4 Look, here comes Lottery, the Prince's Messenger. He should know.

Lottery *(entering)* Make way, make way, make way.
                          The Prince is here today.
                          Strong and brave, without fear.
                          Let's all give him a great big cheer.

Courtiers *(all)* Hooray! Hooray!

Prince *(entering* Hello everyone. Hello Lottery. *(to audience)* Hello one and all.
   I'm Prince Lionheart, my kingdom stretches from *(local place)* to *(local place)*.
   My Messenger here, Lottery, keeps me in touch with all the news *(to audience)*
   and gives all the local gossip to Nanny - so watch out!

Lottery agrees gleefully

Brrrrr - it's getting colder.

Man in Moon Good evening, Prince Lionheart. I see you are full of winter cheer.
   But I fear it will become even colder yet.

Prince Yes, I hear that the Ice Queen's forces have taken the far lands, and are
   now moving towards us.

Man in Moon Yes, you must save your people from her coldness and her
   wickedness.

Courtiers *(all)* Yes - save us Your Highness.

Prince But how? Nothing anyone has tried so far seems to stop her advance.

Man in Moon You must journey to the 'End of the Rainbow' to find the secret
   of how to stop the Ice Queen. I will help you on your travels and magic will be
   needed, but during the day I am almost powerless for I need my sleep. Yet at
   all times, I will be available if you need me.

Prince Thank you Man in the Moon. As for daytime magic, the Palace Magician,
   that's funny, he is called Rainbow, will help. Lottery, go and fetch Rainbow.

Lottery exits

Man in Moon It will be a perilous journey, through the Black Forest, the
   Murky Marshlands and into the Buttercup Meadows beyond. At least my friend
   the Sun still rules there, although I fear the Ice Queen has now taken parts of
   the marshlands.

Prince I know that with your guidance, and my trusty friends, we can make the
   journey.

Man in Moon The future of your kingdom, and indeed the whole of the world
   as you know it, rests with you, on the success of your mission.

Prince *(defiantly)* We have to succeed.

Lottery *(entering)* Your Highness, the good news or the bad news?

Prince The bad news.

Lottery   I sought him here, I sought him there,
                               I couldn't find him anywhere.

Prince Well, what's the good news?

Lottery   I looked again, it was a pain,
                               He was being chased by the Dame!

Enter Rainbow, running, does not see the Prince who is now inconspicuous at one side towards the back. Rainbow goes to the front of the stage

Rainbow *(to audience)* Hi everyone! Oh dear, Dame Laughalot, the Prince's Nanny, keeps chasing me. She thinks that as I'm the Palace Magician I can simply wave my magic wand and make her beautiful. I've tried so many times to stop her pestering me, but she *(shakes head in despair)*. Anyway *(brightly)* bet you can't guess who I am. That's right, I'm Rainbow the Palace Magician. *(composes himself)* Look at all my wonderful colours, oh, I'm a bright thing all right. Do you know how many colours are in a Rainbow? Or what the colours are?

Audience Yes/no!

Rainbow *(ad lib here depending on the response, with house lights up a little)* Yes, that's right. There are seven, and seven is supposed to be a lucky number isn't it? Right, the first seven children that can come up here and tell me the seven colours of the Rainbow will be lucky. They can come onto the stage at the end of the pantomime if they would like to. Right, who's first, you, yes, and your colour? *(after a short while)* That's red, orange, yellow, green, blue and violet *(or whatever)* what is the last one? Yes, that's right, indigo, a sort of bright bluey purplish colour. Well done, super. Now don't forget, I'll see all of you later at the end of the pantomime. *(gives each a Rainbow colour card)* Right *(to whole audience)* I know what, just so you all remember who I am, whenever I come on, I'll say 'Hi Everyone', and you can shout 'Hi Rainbow'. Is that OK? Oh goodie, let's have a practice, like all good pantomimes, he he. Right, ready, HI EVERYONE.

Audience Hi Rainbow!

Rainbow Pardon - sorry - didn't quite hear you. You'll have to shout a bit louder, especially you lot at the back. Ready - Hi everyone!

Audience HI RAINBOW!

Rainbow That's better. *(sadly)* I think I'd better let you know - I'm a bit of a failed magician. *(encouraging sympathy from audience)* It's probably because I've only got a little wobbly wand. *(pulls out a wobbly wand and shows it to the audience)* I wish I had a bigger one! *(pause)* Still, *(brightly)* can get some tricks right. I have this magic word that I made up and it seems to work - ABRACADABULOUS - that's from Abracadabra, the magic word, and fabulous, like what I am! Look, I'll show you - ABRACADABULOUS *(swirls cape around and performs a simple trick. One can usually be obtained from an appropriate shop in town. Alternatively, by waving a 'magic' silk scarf around, then pushing tightly into one hand, the other hand can appear to make the scarf turn into a bunch of flowers pulled down from the sleeve and shown to the audience. Putting the scarf in a pocket at a convenient moment later)* I hear the Prince is looking for me. I wonder what he wants?

Prince *(who has been watching Rainbow's antics, now comes forward)* Ah Rainbow, there you are.

Rainbow *(surprised)* OH! Your Highness. *(bows)*

Prince Up to your trickery tricks again. Now look here, when I asked you to conjure up for me a bride, and you said you could arrange for a bird to be by my side - this is not what I expected! *(holds up a naked chicken, received whilst standing by the wings, and kept hidden)*

Rainbow *(giggling)* Failed again!

Prince *(throwing chicken to side)* Seriously now, you know that the Ice Queen is freezing the lands in the north, well, she is now moving down to my kingdom. According to the Man in the Moon, the only way to stop her is to find the secret at the 'End of the Rainbow', and funnily enough that's your name isn't it!

Rainbow Yes, and there's no secret at my end *(looking behind him)* and even if there is, you're not going to find it!

Prince *(laughs)* No, not your end Rainbow, the secret is at the 'Rainbow's End'.

Rainbow *(a little confused)* Oh?

Prince The rainbow in the sky! Oh never mind, I'll explain later. We've got to go and find Nanny before our expedition. *(looks up)* See you later Man in the Moon.

Man in Moon Yes Prince, you must prepare well, and I suppose I had better start work, permanent night shift. Still, at least I can see everything that goes on from up here.

Prince *(leaving with all on stage, rubbing hands and looking around)* Brrr, it's getting colder, come on everyone, let's go and warm ourselves up.

Lights fade a little on stage, music starts, and spotlights focus towards the back of the audience, where Jack Frost and his little Frosties (all in silver) enter through the audience, creeping, sneaking and perhaps hissing, until they get to the stage

Jack Frost Ah ha! Let's spread a little coldness here.

Jack and a few others can have small spray cans of Christmas Tree silver/ tinsel and spray a little around the stage. Not suggested on the audience, unless in appropriate cases

Jack Frost Oh I do like working for the Ice Queen. She always lets me go in front to explore. That's it my little Frosties, just a little colder whilst no-one is about. *(laughs)*

The Man in the Moon is watching, looking most concerned

I think I should tell the Ice Queen about this lovely Palace, she can freeze it and live here herself. *(to audience)* She's just gone for the weekend to Iceland, a working break. *(pulls out a mobile phone and dials)* Hi Queenie, Jack Frost here. *(listens)* Well cool down a bit, sorry to interrupt your holiday, but I've found a wonderful Palace for you. *(listens)* Right, we'll come and meet you, and I can show you the way. *(puts aerial down and replaces mobile)* Come on Frosties, we must go and meet the Queen. She's coming back on the next iceberg.

All exit. A few courtiers enter

Courtier 1 Oh it's a lot colder now. Look at the ice and snow.

Courtier 2 I know the Prince can save us from the horrible Ice Queen.

Courtier 3 The Man in the Moon said he can.

Courtier 4 And the Prince's Nanny, Dame Laughalot, can help. She's taught him lots of things.

Courtier 5 Yes she has. Oh look, here she comes now.

Courtiers *(all)* Here comes Dame Laughalot.

Laughalot *(enters loudly dressed, laughing nearly all the time)* Hello, hello, hello. *(turns)* Goodbye, goodbye. *(turns back laughing)* Just joking! Silly me! Oh hello girls and boys, and mums and dads. Oh sorry, mums and dads, you're all children tonight aren't you? Oooo, I see some of you have brought your pets with you. I can see a little monkey down there, yes you. And there's a funny bunny over there. Isn't it funny, a rabbit's a bunny, turn him over and tickle his tummy. Put him back. Ha ha ha. Oh dear, I just can't stop laughing. That's how I got my name you know, Dame Laughalot. I look in the mirror and laugh and laugh. So would you if you had a face like mine. Oh I felt a little chill when I came on, did you feel a little chill? *(hitches up her knickers)* Well, leave it alone! Oh, I'm frozen to the bones I am. Makes you shiver and wobble, doesn't it? Oh I've got the wobbles. Would you like to see my wobbles? I bet you would. *(appropriate gestures)* But you can't. *(pause)* Perhaps I'll show you later. And you sir, you look like a gentleman who could warm me up a bit. Ohhh, I used to be hot you know. Hot stuff that is. If it gets any colder we could all freeze. Did you know that the human body is 98% water? It is you know, and if that wicked Ice Queen gets her way. *(aside)* I wish I could get mine. It means that we could all freeze except just that little bit of us. *(holds her fingers together with a little space between)* Oh I wonder what little bit of me wouldn't freeze? I suppose you'd be alright wouldn't you sir? *(points to previously mentioned man)* Oh I think we should all have something to warm us up, don't you? Yes, well I haven't got anything, what a shame. Ahhh, I know, I wonder if the Palace Magician could help. Do you think he could? *(hitches up her knickers)*

Audience Yes!

Laughalot Yes, I thought you would. *(sweetly but loudly)* Rainbow, dearest. *(to audience)* I keep asking him to wave his wand at me - I do - I want him to wave his wand at me and make me happy! Oh he could make me so happy. He thinks I want to be beautiful, but I already am, aren't I? Yes. Who said no? You fibber. Anyway, all I want is him, my toy boy! Ooooo Rainbow dearest, come here sweetie. Bring something to warm me up.

Rainbow *(entering carrying a mug, making out he doesn't want to spill any)* Hi everyone!

Audience HI RAINBOW!

Rainbow Here you are Dame Laughalot.

Laughalot *(all gooey and giggly-ish)* Well that's not what I was hoping for. But never mind, what is it?

Rainbow Hot chocolate, drinking chocolate, hot chocolate ...

Laughalot That won't do. How can I share this *(takes mug)* with everyone? I can't throw it to them, they'll all get wet. Oh, I don't know though. Would you like some hot chocolate? Good. Here it comes. *(throws the nil-contents at the audience)* Fooled you, he he. Now come on Rainbow, can't you use your magic to create something nice that we can share with everyone?

Rainbow Well I'll try. Hmm. A little magic. *(produces his wobbly wand)*

Laughalot *(perplexed)* How long has it been like that?

Rainbow That's as long as it's ever been. *(waves wand and swirls cape)* ABRACADABULOUS! *(lots of different mints fall from an open bag hidden inside his cape)*

Courtiers help to pick them up

Laughalot Ah, wonderful, mints. Oh, now just look at that, a Fox's Glacier Mint. Picture of a fox on a glacier. Now that's silly isn't it - there should be a polar bear on a glacier shouldn't there? Yes. I'll keep one of these because I'm a Foxy Lady. Oooooo. *(hitches up her knickers)* Rainbow, take some of these to the children at the back, whilst I look after this lot.

Rainbow goes to back of the audience. House lights up, or spotlights on, as he works his way to the front of the stage, and Dame throws mints to the front areas. Rainbow can carry extra sweets in his pockets and 'conjure' up a few from an ear or two etc., Dame continues through this with

That's it Rainbow. *(to all)* Those at the back are from *(local rough area)* They only pay half price (or, 'we give them 10p each to come here to fill up the hall') You lot in the middle are, I suppose, from *(local area)* and *(poshly)* of course, you lot in the front here are from *(local posh area)* This lot always get the front seats. Thank you Rainbow. *(to audience)* That's yer lot.

Rainbow *(now back on stage)* Well must be off and get ready for the Prince. See you later. *(exits)*

Laughalot Oh, he's such a lovely young man. Oh if only I could make magic with him. I could wobble his wobbly wand for ever. Ooooooooooo.

Song No 2

'I Wanna Be Rainbow's Girl' to music of 'Bobby's Girl'. Music starts and juveniles come on to dance a rock or twist style, dressed either in aerobic or body outfits, all the same colour, or preferably, if available, outfits like 'Cheerleaders or Twirletts'. They can also sing, if thought appropriate, with the Dame, who leads off. The song finishes, but the music doesn't fade and starts again. Dame goes towards the band/music person

Laughalot Oi, stop! Stop! What are you playing at? We've finished!

Band/Music I didn't know. No body told me.

Laughalot Well I had finished. Didn't you read the script, you idiot?
Band/Music Yes, but …

*General 'threatening' banter back and forth. Dame unplugs leads and/or takes
an instrument, if acceptable, ending with*

Band/Music Oh, get back up there and get on with it.
Laughalot Well you get it right in future! *(to audience, sweetly)* Sorry about
that. *(looks menacingly at Band/Music then back to audience sweetly and
coyly, perhaps a little embarrassed)* You may have noticed me hitching up my
(mouths to audience, and points to her knickers) Knickers now and again. Yes,
my knickers, and for those who didn't hear at the back, I said *(shouts)*
KNICKERS. They don't make elastic like they used to, look. *(lifts up skirt to
reveal eccentric pair of bloomers with loose elastic)* They sometimes fall down.
Most embarrassing for a lady you know. I wonder if you could help me. If you
see my knickers fall down, will you tell me please?
Audience YES!
Laughalot You will, good. Thank you. I know, just shout knickers, or bloomers
if you're a bit embarrassed or shy. Will that be alright?
Audience YES!
Laughalot Thank you. Now you will remember won't you? Shout knickers, and
I'll know what you mean. Well tatty bye now, must go and get my Hottie Bottie.
Bye, bye.

Dame and courtiers exit, and as Dame goes out she lets her knickers fall

Audience Knickers!
Laughalot Oh dear, already, thank you.

Dame exits hoisting up her knickers, and Prince, Rainbow and Lottery enter

Prince Nanny will join us when she has filled her bottle.
Rainbow That's funny, she's normally emptying it.
Prince *(jovially)* No Rainbow, not the sherry bottle, her hot water bottle.
Man in Moon Prince Lionheart, whilst you were gone, the advance party of the
Ice Queen, led by that rascal Jack Frost, was here. See the ice? He has informed
her about your Palace. She wants to freeze it and live here herself.
Prince Then we must make haste. What shall we do?
Man in Moon You and your party must travel through the Black Forest where
the Mibbie Mibbies live. Fearless little imps that have formed an alliance with
the Ice Queen. She has little need of the forests. The Mibbie Mibbies nip and
bite, and although not really dangerous, they will try to slow you down.
Rainbow We can always nip and bite them!
Man in Moon They will be too quick for you. At the end the forest are the Murky
Marshlands. The Ice Queen has already frozen most of these. You must wrap
up well, and thick boots or your toes will freeze.
Lottery   I am fleet of foot, or so I am told.
               My little toes will never get cold.

Prince That's as maybe, but take heed of what the Man in the Moon tells us.

Man in Moon The villagers on the edge of the marshlands will guide you. Do not stray from the paths, for in places the ice will be thin, and there is death in the bogs below. It will be best to wait for daybreak. Beyond the marshlands are Buttercup Meadows. This where you will find your goal.

Rainbow Oh goodie. I like playing footie in the meadow.

Man in Moon This is no time for jesting Rainbow. Unless the Ice Queen is stopped, there will be no more meadows, just a frozen landscape. My friend the Sun still retains control in that region, but the Ice Queen intends to send blizzards that will block out the sky and hide the Sun. There will be no sunshine to make the snow or ice disappear. Magic will be needed to create a Rainbow, whilst the Sun still shines, and at midday when the Sun is strongest, you must create a Rainbow. When it appears you must dig quickly for the secret, but listen carefully - TIME STANDETH STILL FOR NO MAN - remember that well Your Highness, and be wise at all times, as I have taught you. The secret will only be revealed to you, one of Royal Blood.

Prince What do we do then?

Man in Moon Return to your Kingdom before nightfall for that is when the Queen plans to attack your Palace. We can tackle her together, destroy her power forever.

Laughalot *(entering carrying hot water bottle and other things)* Sorry I'm late. *(comes close to Rainbow and giggles)* I've only got my Hottie Bottie to keep me warm, for now.

Rainbow moves away, nervously

Prince That's alright Nanny, we have our plan, come, let's get ready for our journey.

Man in Moon You must leave soon, for I fear there is not much time, and a long way to go.

As they all exit

Wait Rainbow, a few moments.

Rainbow *(staying behind as others all go off)* What is it Man in the Moon?

Man in Moon Along the way, some magic will be needed that you with your wobbly wand can perform, but should you ever need my help during the day, when the Sun is at its highest, I cannot be woken except by - come closer Rainbow - you should *(whispers to Rainbow, who listens intently and somewhat confused)* Have you got it?

Rainbow sort of nods

Repeat it to me.

Rainbow whispers back

Good, now off you go with your friends.

Rainbow exits. Music starts and Jack Frost enters, slowly and stealthily, with some of his Frosties. Some through the audience if preferred

Jack Frost Good, nobody about. It's OK Your Majesty.

Enter Ice Queen to menacing music, striding. Three Frosties guarding her

Ice Queen Ah ha young Jack, you have done well indeed to find such a magnificent Palace, worthy of me *(emphatically)* THE ICE QUEEN. Ah Ha Ha. I shall rule my frozen kingdom *(emphatically)* AND THE WHOLE WORLD FROM HERE!

The Man in the Moon is watching, as the Ice Queen is strutting around, and the Frosties are darting about with ice sprays

Jack Frost Thank you Your Majesty. When shall we start 'the big freeze'?
Ice Queen Soon Jack, soon, but look here. *(to front of audience)* Kiddie Winkies! I just love Kiddie Winkies. They're so easy to make cold, and to freeze their little fingers. Instead of fish fingers for tea, we can have Kiddie Winkie fingers. Ah Ha Ha! *(menacingly)* I'm going to freeze you all. Turn you into little blocks of ice. Ice cubies. Ah Ha Ha.
Audience Oh no you're not!
Ice Queen Oh yes I am.
Audience Oh no you're not!
Ice Queen OH YES I AM.
Audience OH NO YOU'RE NOT!
Ice Queen We'll soon see about that. Jack, show them how.

Some of the Frosties have brought on a 'giant' spray can. Jack gets this and starts towards the audience

Ice Queen No Jack. We'll leave them until later. We have other tasks first. What is the situation here?
Jack Frost *(giving can to Frosties)* The people, they are full of hope that you will not succeed with your plans. They look to their Prince to save them.
Ice Queen Ah, they are but mere peasants, and I fear nothing from the Prince. *(loudly)* THERE IS NO-ONE WHO CAN STOP ME. AH HA HA! *(to audience)* No there isn't. Go and get sunburnt whilst you still can. HA ha ha.
Rainbow *(entering nonchalantly, not seeing the Ice Queen, but then, suddenly)* No, not you. *(shouts)* THE ICE QUEEN IS HERE ALREADY!
Ice Queen There is no use shouting. The end is inevitable. There is nothing you can do to stop my plans.
Rainbow Oh yes there is. *(produces his wobbly wand, swirls his cape, and produces an old blow torch, or box of matches)* ABRACADABULOUS. With this I can melt you and your cronies.
Ice Queen You and your silly magic. You think you can stop me with that? FREEZE IT JACK.

Jack darts across and freezes the blow torch with his normal spray, or the large 'spray' used in conjunction with his normal spray. Rainbow looks at it, somewhat dejected

Rainbow *(sadly)* Failed again. *(confidently)* But the Prince and the Man in the Moon have plans to destroy you.

Ice Queen Ah, I will deal with them when I have rested from my holiday - a wonderful time, but the journey home was rather long and tiring. The iceberg had to be diverted via the North Pole, *(contemptuously)* due to a SUNNY DAY! But I will leave you with a taste of what is to come - Jack *(points to Rainbow)* make him shiver a little. Ha ha ha ha.

Jack sprays some ice/snow on Rainbow who starts to shiver more and more. The Frosties jump up and down gleefully

Jack!

Ice Queen beckons Jack to the front of the stage and 'whispers' to him, so that she thinks only the audience can hear, but the Man in the Moon is still above

The Man in the Moon is powerful and magical, but I have weakened his powers by *(emphasising)* freezing his entourage, his pets. Ha ha ha. His sloppy cat, his dopey dog and that clumsy cow. They are all frozen solid, and I have put them in a place where they can never be found. Ha ha. *(loudly)* Now come, for by tomorrow night the Prince's Palace and his Kingdom will be mine. Ha ha ha. *(as going off)* I'll send you a little snow later, just to cool the place down a bit. Ha ha. And Jack, make sure that the villages in the Marshlands suffer a little more, before I take them completely. Ha ha ha.

All exit, and Dame Laughalot enters, sort of running

Laughalot Ah there you are Rainbow. I heard your shouting. I've been looking ... *(stops and stares)* Whatever is the matter?

Rainbow remains silent, still shivering

Oh you're so cold. *(concerned, but really happy)* Let me cuddle you. Oh, you'll love my cuddles. *(there is nothing Rainbow can do as she cuddles him all over)* Actually you are very cold to cuddle. How about this? *(starts placing hot water bottle on various parts of Rainbow's anatomy. Starting to thaw out, he reacts accordingly)* There, that's better isn't it? *(to audience)* See, all you lot out there with electric blankets and central heating. Don't know what you're missing, do you?

Rainbow Yes. Stop it. Thank you. Enough. That'll do etc., *(starts backing off a little)* It was that wicked Ice Queen, oh she's so nasty and evil. She makes everyone cold. She has a horrible laugh. She's going to freeze the Palace and take over the Kingdom. And she's even threatened to eat the children.

Laughalot *(to audience)* And that's just her good points.

Rainbow She and Jack Frost were here, and those nasty little Frosties. She said she was coming back soon. I must tell the Prince. *(starts to go, comes back, kisses Dame on cheek)* Thank you for everything. If there's anything I can do for you?

Dame stands dumbstruck as her knickers fall down. Rainbow exits, not noticing

Audience KNICKERS!

Laughalot Anything he can do for me. I'll say there is. He can do anything for me. *(dreamily hoists up knickers, then back to reality)* Oh thank you. *(dreams again)*

Song No 3

Dame sings, 'I'm H A P P Y'

Laughalot   I'm H A P P Y. I'm H A P P Y.
                  I'm sure I am, I know I am. I'm H A P P Y.
                  (to audience) Would you like to sing as well?

Audience Yes/No!

Laughalot Oh goodie. It's so easy. *(or, 'oh please just once, to share my happiness/ well you're going to')* Ready? After three - one, two, three ...

Audience and **Laughalot**
                  I'm H A P P Y. I'm H A P P Y.
                  I'm sure I am, I know I am. I'm H A P P Y.

Laughalot Oh well done. There, easy wasn't it? Must go and make Rainbow happy now. Byeeee. Oh Rainbow! Cooeee, where are you? *(exits waving to audience and looking excited)*

Prince *(entering slowly and thinking)* Oh what am I to do? I have a marvellous magician, a loyal and lucky messenger, and *(laughing)* an adorable Nanny. And of course my good and faithful people. But I have no-one with whom to share my Palace and Kingdom. To share my life with - a bride. I know I must deal with the Ice Queen first, but I wish I had someone of my own to fight for.

Music starts. The Prince stops suddenly as a 'Falling Star' is seen. Either a juvenile, or a cut-out star falling down a piece of twine

Man in Moon Your Highness, one should always make a wish when you see a falling star.

Prince Yes, a wish.

He wishes. Gentle music comes up. One side of the stage snowflakes begin to fall. (snow spray or cotton wool) From the wings a few snowflakes, dressed all in white, start 'fluttering' in. Amongst them is Snowflake. As she is dancing the Prince looks at her and is transfixed. Snowflake sees the Prince at the same time, stops and looks lovingly at him

My wish - came true.

The Man in the Moon is smiling. The Prince looks up at him and smiles too, then looks back at Snowflake. They move towards each other and hold hands centre stage. The other snowflakes gather round, and a few courtiers come on from the opposite side of the snowfall (if required). Music starts and with the Prince leading off, they sing

Song No 4

'Blue Moon' or 'Moonlight Becomes You'. As the music fades at the end of the song, Snowflake goes to retreat, with the other snowflakes, to where the snow fell, but the Prince stops her

Prince Who are you?

Snowflake *(thoughtfully, yet lovingly)* I am a Snow Maiden. A snowflake that falls, and dances in the winds that blow. And who are you?

Prince I am Prince Lionheart. But you are not just a snowflake, you are lovely. My wish came true. Won't you stay here, with me, in my Palace?

Snowflake You live here? In this wonderful Palace? Oh how I would love to stay here with you, but as a snowflake, *(sadly)* I go wherever I am sent. I am here now only as a flurry, and cannot stay long. *(confidently)* But I believe I will be here again soon, for the snowstorms are to be sent tomorrow night, to cover all the lands, and then I will be able to stay with you forever.

Prince *(exasperated)* What am I to do? I fell in love with you the moment I saw you, and the only way for us to be together is to let the wicked Ice Queen take over my Palace and Kingdom.

Snowflake looks at the Prince, somewhat startled and yet sad by what he has said. The Prince does not see her concern, as he is looking upwards, turning around with arms outstretched, despondently

If I let that happen, then my people and I could all perish. At best we would survive on a cold and desolate world, without warmth, love and romance. What can be done?

Man in Moon *(serenely)* Do not worry Prince Lionheart, all will be well in the end, after your quest.

Prince But how?

Man in Moon Do you doubt the power of my wisdom or my magic? My whole life is to look after you and your world, to look after the warmth of your souls.

Prince Oh no Man in the Moon, you are so clever, so good. I could never doubt you.

Man in Moon Then believe in me for I know things that cannot yet be revealed. Trust me.

Prince *(turning to Snowflake)* To find you now, and yet to lose you so soon. Must you go yet?

Snowflake I must. Even the warmth of your heart and love is melting me now.   *SoNG*

Icicle *(entering with a swagger, wearing icy 'shades')* Like Hi Snowflake. This is a 'cool' place, and who's the handsome fellah?

Snowflake Oh Icicle it's you. This is Prince Lionheart. He lives here in his Palace.

Icicle Hey, smooth pad man. Like let's 'party' on Saturday night. By then I should be 'hang-ing around'.

Snowflake *(to Prince)* This is Icicle. She is a bit wayout, but she is my best friend, and so much fun. *(questioningly)* I'm sure you would get to like her in time?

Prince *(somewhat disapproving)* Well, yes, perhaps.

Icicle Wanna hang around some Snowflake, get to know the Princie better? Know what I mean?

Snowflake Oh yes Icicle. *(sees Prince looking puzzled)* We can be together a little longer if I cling to Icicle. Her coldness transfers to me. Come on, hold hands. *(Snowflake holds hands with Icicle and Prince, laughing)* I hope I don't make you too cold.

Prince *(dreamily)* I shall never feel cold when I am with you.

Icicle Yeuk Princie. Hey Snowflake, let's ramble the grounds, see if 'Flash Jack' is about.

Prince cringes at the first remark, and is surprised at the last one

Prince This 'Flash Jack', is he Jack Frost, the Ice Queen's protégé?

Snowflake Yes.

Prince Well I certainly don't want to meet him. He's almost as bad as the Ice Queen.

Icicle Hey no Princie. He's the best groover in the land. He and I just sli-de together. We're almost an 'item'.

Snowflake He's a rascal. He doesn't really mean any harm. It's just that I think he likes the power that *(hesitates)* that the Ice Queen gives him. I think he wants to take over from her one day.

Prince Not if I can help it! Anyway, we'll deal with that later, come, let us be together for a while. *(looks around)* I must be back soon, the others will be waiting for me.

Icicle Hey, I've gotta come too, else Snowflake, you'll simply me-lt under his caresses.

Snowflake Yes, come then, and you too snowflakes.

All exit, Prince, Snowflake and Icicle holding hands. Enter Rainbow, Dame Laughalot, and Lottery who is holding a lamp and a small pack. Dame is holding her bag and a blanket rolled up. Rainbow is holding two small packs, his, and one for the Prince

Rainbow Hi everyone!

Audience HI RAINBOW!

Laughalot *(looking through her bag, holding items up)* Well, that's me ready. Hottie Bottie, Sherry Bottie and Pill Bottie. *(looks behind her, shows audience and pats it)* And my Big Bottie. Ha ha ha.

Rainbow Has anyone seen the Prince? He said we had to go and get ready quickly. And we're here and he isn't.

Man in Moon Be patient a moment Rainbow. He is happy and yet sad. He knows the need for urgency, and will be with you soon.

Enter Palace courtiers

Courtier 1 We have come to bid you well on your mission.
Courtier 2 Our hearts and prayers go with you.

Prince returns, a little sad

Laughalot Oh, what's the matter my little Princiekins?
Prince Oh Dame Laughalot, I have just met the girl of my dreams. I saw a falling star. I wished, and my wish came true.
Laughalot *(looking round)* Where, where?
Prince She has gone now.
Laughalot No no, I mean the falling star. I want to make a wish. *(coyly)* For me and Rainbow.
Prince Don't worry Nanny, I'm sure your wishes will come true one day.
Laughalot I suppose so. *(to front stage)* Perhaps I should read my stars. *(looks up, all round, round and round, then dizzy, knickers fall down, staggers about)*
Audience KNICKERS!
Laughalot Thank you. *(hoists them up)* I can't make any sense of that lot up there. *(quickly)* I'll read The Sun in the morning - much brighter! Anyway, *(turns to Prince excitedly)* tell me of this girl, where did you meet her, where does she live, what does she look like, what …?
Prince *(now composed, and more jovial)* Wait, wait. I will tell you all on our journey, for we must now make haste.
Rainbow All is ready for our expedition Your Highness.
Prince Well done. *(looking around)*
Rainbow And the good people of the Palace have come to bid us success with our quest.
Courtier 3 Good luck Your Highness.
Courtier 4 We know you can bring back the secret.
Courtier 5 Yes, the secret of how to destroy the wicked Ice Queen.
Rainbow And I won't be frightened, not of the darkness in the Black Forest, not of the Mibbie Mibbies that nip and bite, nor of the frozen murky marshlands, not even of that nasty Ice Queen herself. *(confidently)* I'm not chicken - SO THERE!
Prince *(heartily)* Well said my good friend. Come then, you lead the way Lottery.

Whilst the Prince has been saying these words, Lottery is pointing to Rainbow and laughing and saying, 'Him not chicken, huh'. He then does a walkaround the stage doing a chicken act, head jerk, bent knees and scuffing with feet, with jacket off shoulders, if applicable. The others are watching and laughing. Rainbow is taking offence

Prince That's enough Lottery. I'm sure Rainbow is as brave as any of us. Come my friends, we must be on our way.

Courtiers gather round the travellers and start to cheer

Lottery *(back to normal)*
> Let us sing a song as we go along.
> Passing through this merry throng.

Laughalot You suggest one Lottery, as you're the rhyming poet. *(sarcastically, yet happily to the audience)* And doesn't he know it. Ha ha.

Lottery *(realization, points finger in the air)* I know. ~~Here we go!~~

Be back soon

Music starts, and Lottery leads off through the courtiers followed by the Prince, Dame Laughalot and Rainbow, all singing. Courtiers move to the back of the stage and perform a series of 'Mexican Waves' whilst still singing. Lottery etc., march round the stage singing (encouraging the audience to sing as well) Suggest twice round the stage before they exit

Everybody - Walk on **Song No 5**

'Here We Go, Here We Go, Here We Go' or 'Walk On, Walk On'. *As they exit at the end of the song the Dame's knickers fall down*

Audience KNICKERS!

Curtain

Scene 2

Journey to the Black Forest Pathway. This is a mini-routine that may be used if the scene change is expected to take a little longer than usual. The four travellers enter front of curtains, walking across the stage as they are still quite brisk at this time

Prince We have done well. We will rest shortly.
Rainbow How about another song? Any ideas anyone?

They stop centre stage. Dame says the first line, then sings

Song No 6

'I Know A Song That'll Get On Your Nerves'

Laughalot
> I know a song that'll get on your nerves,
> Get on your nerves, get on your nerves.
> I know a song that'll get on your nerves,
> Get, get, get on your nerves.

All
> Oh, we know a song that'll get on your nerves,
> Get on your nerves, get on your nerves.
> We know a song that'll get on your nerves,
> Get, get, get on your nerves.

Now encouraging the audience to join in

All/Audience   We know a song that'll get on your nerves,
                      Get on your nerves, get on your nerves.
                      We know a song that'll get on your nerves,
                      Get, get, get on your nerves.
Laughalot *(stops everyone, waving hands at audience etc.)* Oh shut-up! You
lot are getting on my nerves. *(pause)* Come on, let's go.
Prince We can't go. They might not have finished changing the scenery yet.
Rainbow Well, have a look.

*Lottery pokes his head through the curtains, pulls his head back and shakes
it, indicating another minute*

Laughalot Well, I'm not staying here. I'll soon be a nervous wreck!
Prince Come on, just another couple of verses.

*Starts to sing again, encouraging audience. Dame sings first line, then whilst
looking around to see if anyone is watching, starts to sneak off on tiptoe,
waving her arms to encourage the audience to keep singing. Puts her finger to
her mouth to indicate 'don't tell anyone'. The others watch her, then they too
sneak off, indicating to the audience to keep singing. After they are off, a loud
'PST' is heard from behind the curtains, then another 'PSSSST - You can come
off now'. Then a stagehand head appears through the curtains looking around
with puzzled expression. (can actually come out and look around) He disappears
back through the curtains, 'They're not out there' is loudly whispered, followed
by, 'Well I don't know, we'd better get on with the pantomime*

Note: *Whilst this gives the stagehands extra time, it does mean that the
players get little respite as they only have a very short time before their entrance
in the next scene. No doubt they will be enjoying it, and will be eager to proceed*

Scene 2a

*The Black Forest Pathway. Curtains open to reveal a frontcloth depicting the
dark forest. Lowish lighting should be used, with spotlights switched on when
the travellers are camped, and Lottery 'makes' light. Due to the forest thickness
it is suggested that only a half moon is projecting from the wings (Man in the
Moon is not in this scene). Enter the travellers with packs etc., slowly, and
looking somewhat weary, Lottery first, followed by the Prince, Dame Laughalot
(hitching up her knickers) and then Rainbow who is looking around quite
frightened. Lottery is holding the lamp*

Laughalot Oh, I'm so tired. Can't we stop and have that rest now?
Prince Yes of course. It's been a difficult journey so far, and we should get a
little sleep before our long day tomorrow.
Laughalot It's so dark. Look, we can only just see the moon through all these
trees. It's alright for Lottery, he's got the lamp.

Rainbow Well what about me? I'm at the back, I know I said that I wouldn't be frightened, but I keep hearing things behind.
Prince Lottery my loyal friend, what say you?
Lottery   I look to the left, and I look to the right.
                                      A camp here *(points down)* would seem alright.

All stop abruptly, centre stage. Prince is treading on the Dame's right foot

Laughalot Right oh!
Prince We'll light a fire to warm us up.
Laughalot Right oh!
Prince Come on, let's get some wood.
Laughalot Right oh!
Prince Are you training a parrot or something?
Laughalot No! You're standing on my right toe.
Prince Oh, sorry Nanny. *(gets off her foot)*

Dame hops around nursing her right foot

Let's get the fire started.
Laughalot Not me. My toe hurts and I'm too tired. I'm going to flop down. Come here Rainbow, you can keep me warm.
Rainbow *(quickly says, and backs away)* I'll get the sticks.
Prince That's a good fellow. Come on Nanny, let's make you comfortable.

Prince helps Dame settle down on her blanket and rubs her foot whilst Rainbow collects a few sticks. He keeps looking around, hearing noises. The Mibbie Mibbies (a few at this time) sneak about at the sides, and pop their heads through the tree holes (flaps) to frighten Rainbow

Rainbow Oh! What was that?
Prince Probably the wind.
Laughalot *(indignantly)* It wasn't me you know.
Rainbow And it wasn't the wind either. *(moves to centre of the camp with the twigs and secretly hides a small torch/lamp with a red cover underneath)*
Laughalot Oh it's cold. Hurry up and light the fire.
Rainbow *(takes the lamp and 'lights' the fire by switching it on, but the lamp goes out)* Oh dear, we seem to have run out of oil. Never mind, the fire's alight now. Here Nanny, warm your hands on that. *(points to fire)*
Laughalot *(coyly)* Oh Rainbow, I'd rather warm my hands somewhere else.

They are all sitting now as creepy music comes up, and the Mibbie Mibbies (more of them) are getting a bit more daring, nearly up to the group

Rainbow What was that? There is something out there. *(spots one)* Oh! *(quaking)* Look, there it is.

All look round but the Mibbie Mibbies have gone back to the sides/tree holes

Prince I can't see anything Rainbow. Come on, settle down.

All look around nervously

Laughalot It's so dark we can't see out there. I would feel safer if it was a bit lighter. Can't we relight the lamp?
Prince I think this calls for another bit of magic Rainbow.
Rainbow I'm too frightened to do any magic.
Lottery There is a way to make things bright.
  Without the lamp we can have light.
Rainbow Well I'm not going out there to collect glow-worms!
Lottery Now all put your hands up in the air.
  Do as I say *(pause as they do so)* and don't despair.
Rainbow *(to audience)* And you lot. Come on everyone. Hands in the air. That's it.

Spotlights now come onto the camp. (if available, the lights are on a dimmer switch, thus, as the lights get brighter, encourage the audience to put their hands higher, thus making the light increase)

Lottery I bet you thought I was a bit of a berk.
  But see, many hands make light work.
Prince Well done Lottery. That should keep the Mibbie Mibbies away. Now come on, let's get some sleep whilst we can.
Rainbow Now listen here Lottery, I'm the magician, don't take liberties.
Laughalot *(sitting up)* I wish someone - anyone - would take liberties with me. *(looking into audience)* Is that gentleman still there in the audience? *(peering)* Cooee. Oh look, he's nearly asleep. We'll have to liven this pantomime up a bit.
Prince I know, let's have a camp-fire sing-song. Come on Nanny, you used to sing me to sleep when I was little.

All sitting up again. The Mibbie Mibbie are at the sides, peering out, now looking interested

Laughalot Oh yes, goodie, singing makes me happy. A nice slow dreamy song.
Prince Well, what shall we sing?
Lottery There is a song that many used to know.
  But it doesn't rhyme, and it isn't slow.
Prince *(laughing)* Well old chap, how does it go?

Song No 7

Lottery Ging Gang Gooley Gooley Gooley Gooley Watch yer,
  Ging Gang Goo, Ging Gang Goo.
  Ging Gang Gooley Gooley Gooley Gooley Watch yer,
  Ging Gang Goo, Ging Gang Goo.

Hey la - Hey la Shay la -. Hey La Sha La Hey La - oooh,
Hey La, Hey La Shay La. Hey La Shay La Hey La Shay La - oooh.

Third verse if required

Shally Wally, Shally Wally, Shally Wally,
Oompah - Oompah - Oompah.

*Then revert back to Ging Gang Gooley etc., Lottery sings the first line, then the
others join in, and encourage the audience too. Suggest only a couple of verses,
then repeat the first if appropriate, getting quicker*

Laughalot Oh that was fun. I'm tired now.
Prince Good. We must all get some rest now. An early start in the morning.
Lottery   Good Night. Good Night.
                  Hope the Mibbie Mibbies don't bite.
                  Nite Nite. Nite Nite.
Rainbow All right Lottery, don't overdo it!
Laughalot Night Night Rainbow. *(snuggles up to him)*

*To creepy music the Mibbie Mibbies now come out up to the sleeping snoring
travellers, and start to nip and bite them. The group, still asleep, start twitching
and 'swatting' the Mibbie Mibbies off without wakening. This can be quite a
funny sketch as they all twitch and swat, suddenly awakening (by a quiet
whisper of 'now') and all sit bolt upright. The Mibbie Mibbies quickly dart back
to the sides/tree holes*

All What was that?
Rainbow *(to audience)* Did you see anything?
Audience Yes, Mibbie Mibbies!
Laughalot What was it? The Mibbie Mibbies?
Audience Yes, Mibbie Mibbies!
Rainbow Who?
Audience THE MIBBIE MIBBIES!
Rainbow *(frightened)* Not those dreaded Mibbie Mibbies. I'm getting out of here.
Prince Now hold it. It looks like we've frightened them off. I don't suppose we'll
get much sleep after-all, so let's get everything together and move on.

*They all get up and bend down, facing inwards, to pick things up. Four Mibbie
Mibbies sneak up quietly and get behind them, one to each, then pinch the
travellers' bottoms simultaneously*

All OUCH!

*They all straighten up, and start to look round, but the Mibbie Mibbie have
crouched down, and thus are not seen*

Rainbow That hurt. I don't like being pinched.

Laughalot Actually, I quite liked it. I haven't had my bottom pinched in years.
Lottery   Dame Laughalot, I quite liked it too.
                I know what, you pinch me, and I'll pinch you.
Rainbow *(slight jealousy, now warming to the Dame)* Go pinch yourself Lottery.

As Lottery goes to pinch himself, his Mibbie Mibbie leans up and pinches him. Lottery is amazed, looks at one hand then at the other, shakes his head in bewilderment and looks around, sees nothing. They all lean down again to pick up the rest of their things, and the Mibbie Mibbies pinch them again

All OUCH!

They all half fall into each other, and drop their packs etc., Then slowly, all creep to the front of the stage, quivering. The Dame's knickers nearly / half fall down. Some audience may shout 'Knickers'. Dame reacts (ad-lib accordingly) 'Nearly that time / not quite / fooled you this time' etc.,

Laughalot Was that the Mibbie Mibbies again?
Audience Yes!
Rainbow Well where are they now?

Mibbie Mibbies are now standing one behind each traveller, poking their heads round and grinning at the audience

Audience Behind you - Behind you!

Travellers turn round slowly to creepy music, peering into the forest. The Mibbie Mibbies keep close and follow them round

Prince We can't see them. Where are they?
Audience Behind you - Behind you!

They all turn round again

Laughalot I still can't see them. *(hitches up her knickers)*
Audience Behind you - Behind you!
Rainbow I'm frightened.
Prince Enough of this. Let's look all round our camp.

They all troop round looking into the forest. The Mibbie Mibbies are giggling and have fallen in behind them

All Can't see them/No sign of them/Not here etc.,
Audience Behind you - Behind you!

Travellers return to front of stage. Mibbie Mibbies are one behind each again

Laughalot *(confidently)* They must have gone. *(to audience)* They're not still here are they?

Audience Yes/Behind you!

Mibbie Mibbies now pinch them all

All OUCH! *(they turn round to see the Mibbie Mibbies)* Ahhh.

They all turn and run around with a Mibbie Mibbie behind each pinching/ biting their bottoms. A sort of 'Knees up' run to 'Knees up Mother Brown' music as they all shout

All We're going/Not staying here/Let's get out/Not the nasty Mibbie Mibbies etc.,

Prince and Lottery run off through sides and escape. Rainbow and Dame (grabs her bag) run off stage (Dame hitches up knickers) and through the audience. House lights up or spotlights. They are followed by two or four Mibbie Mibbies. Curtain comes down to allow next scene change to be completed. Dame, Rainbow and Mibbie Mibbies all end up back on stage. The first two briefly stand aghast/ trembling before exiting through the curtains followed by the Mibbie Mibbies. This is necessary or the audience may be confused at which point to applaud, most likely on the final exit if this approach is taken. Also, it may be worth while for the Prince and Lottery to come out and shout to their friends, 'This way/Here' etc., and exit back through curtains just as friends reach the stage

Curtain

Scene 3

Village on the edge of Murky Marshlands. Backcloth in silvers, whites, ice blues and blacks, for immediate impact. Lighting can be white or blue, with possibly some UV lighting included. The Moon is silvery, and the Man in the Moon is sitting up watching, in the same position as in the first set. The general scene depicts part of a village, with the edge of the forest on one side, and murky marshlands in the background. Most aspects are covered in ice/snow

Jack Frost and Icicle enter and move to centre stage as he takes her hand. Some snowflakes and frosties, spraying a little ice, are around. They all dance (open/slow/graceful) to, and sing (possibly assisted by adult chorus hidden behind the wings)

Song No 8

They sing, 'By The Light Of The Silvery Moon'. A villager's dog, Trumper, comes out and barks at them

At the end of the song, Jack decides on one more quick spray around the village, then he, holding hands with Icicle, signals everyone off. The villagers then start to appear, stretching and yawning, having been woken by the barking. Villager 1 goes up to Trumper, whilst looking around

Villager 1 What's up old girl? Somebody about?
Trumper Woof, woof! *(looks in the direction that the Frosties went)*

Villagers are all now out and awake

Villager 2 Frost and snow again. When will it ever end? That Ice Queen has a lot to answer for. She does nothing but freeze our lands.
Villager 3 We must destroy her, else we'll not survive.
Villager 4 Nor our children. They shiver all the time now.
Villager 5 The forest wood is too frozen to burn brightly, and nearly all our oil is gone. What are we to do?
Villager 1 Rid ourselves of the wicked Ice Queen of course. Then everything will be well again.
Villager 2 I hear that the Prince is trying to do something. I know he has tried before, but this time he has the Man in the Moon to help him.
Villager 3 And his trusty followers. And we'll help too, won't we?
Villagers *(all)* Yes, yes, we'll help to destroy/kill the Ice Queen.
Villager 4 See, Lottery approaches. Perhaps he has good news.
Villager 5 *(laughing)* And the bad. He'll never change.

Enter Lottery, a little haggard

What news Lottery?
Lottery Do you want the good news or the bad news?

Villagers laugh

Villager 5 Told you so. Come on then Lottery, what's the bad news?
Lottery   We came through the forest in the depth of night.
                 Those Mibbie Mibbies did us all, nip and bite.
                 We fought them off, with all our might.
                 But oh it was a dreadful fright.

Villagers laugh at his actions

Villager 5 Well, what's the good news?
Lottery   We fought and fought, and got away.
                 We live to fight another day.
                 The Prince will be here very soon,
                 He has a mission to complete - at noon.
Villager 1 Here he comes. Welcome Prince Lionheart.

Enter Prince, haggard but quite composed. Villagers gather round the Prince

Villager 2 The snow and ice were here again last night Sire. They come all the time now.

Prince I can see. It appears the Ice Queen has started early. What news do you have for me Man in the Moon?

Man in Moon It is not as bad as it would seem. The Ice Queen sent Jack Frost and his followers here to spread a little frost before she launches her main attack on the Buttercup Meadows, and then your own Kingdom. And yet I believe she will send some snowstorms beforehand, as a taste of what is to come, as is her way.

Prince Then we *(emphatically)* must complete our mission at midday, or we are all doomed.

Man in Moon Indeed you must.

Prince Good villagers, how far is it to the Buttercup Meadows? When will we reach them?

Villager 3 'Tis not far Prince Lionheart. You should be there by 12 o'clock.

Prince Good. Lottery we will wait here a short while, until Rainbow and Nanny catch up. They can't be far away.

Lottery No doubt Sire they will be here soon. Can you see them, Man in the Moon?

Man in Moon *(laughing)* They are still scurrying from the Mibbie Mibbies. But you are right Lottery, they will be here shortly.

Prince Good.

Villager 4 Your Highness, some warm milk for you and your messenger?

Villager 5 And food too?

Prince Thank you my good friends, for we have travelled much of the night, and thirst and hunger prevail. I know your rations are scarce, but can you spare two further portions for Rainbow and my Nanny?

Villager 1 Of course Your Highness.

Villagers 1 and 5 exit

Villager 2 Is it true that you hope to destroy the wicked Ice Queen?

Villager 3 And rid us of her freezing torment forever?

Prince I believe and hope I can, for all my people, my Kingdom, and all the lands.

Man in Moon *(a little apprehensively)* Your Highness, you have yet to complete your task, and, I can but hope that you have learned from my love and wisdom, and indeed from that of your Nanny. You must think carefully what to do, when the secret is revealed to you.

Prince *(querying)* You show hesitancy Man in the Moon. Will I not do the best for my people and ...

Man in Moon *(interrupting)* I am sorry for interrupting Your Highness, and I am sure you *(emphasising)* will do your best, but think back through your life, your childhood, to both the good and bad times. Ponder wisely Prince Lionheart.

Prince begins to think about what the Man in the Moon has said. Villagers look confused by the conversation

Enter Rainbow and Dame Laughalot (with bag) through audience, quite bedraggled

Laughalot Oh dear, oh dear, oh dear. What an awful time.

Rainbow Well at least we reached the village. Look, there's the Prince and Lottery.

Prince *(looking at them, quite concerned)* Oh, hello good friends.

Laughalot What is it? I see the ice all round. Has the Ice Queen started already?

Prince What? Oh, no Nanny. This was a minor attack by Jack Frost. The Man in the Moon says that I must think well and long over my life, and to his and your teachings, before I destroy the Ice Queen.

Rainbow What? The quicker we get rid of her the better.

Villager 4 Yes. We don't want to freeze to death. We want to be cheerful and happy again.

Villager 2 We have suffered enough. You must destroy the wicked Ice Queen.

Prince I hear you well, but the wisdom of the Man in the Moon is great. He has looked over us for all time. His love and warmth, his magic and romance, for us is true. I should listen to him.

Enter Villagers 1 and 5 with chunks of bread and warm milk in 'pots'. Trumper sniffs around. Dame hitches up her knickers

Villager 1 Here you are Your Highness, and for your fellow travellers.

Dame lets her knickers drop

Audience KNICKERS!

Laughalot Whoops a daisy! *(hoisting up her knickers)* For a moment there I thought you had brought me a spare pair of 'smalls'. *(to audience)* Very good. Don't know what I'd do without you.

Prince Hr. Hm. No Nanny. *(to villagers)* Many thanks for your hospitality.

Villager 5 'Tis the least we can do.

Travellers take a chunk and a 'pot' each

Man in Moon Prince Lionheart, a snowstorm approaches, but take little heed for it is only one of the Ice Queen's flurries.

Villager 1 Come inside, before departing through the Murky Marshlands.

Villager 2 Yes, to finish your food and drink, under shelter.

Villager 3 And rest awhile. We have hay and palliasses.

Laughalot *(quickly)* I BEG YOUR PARDON!

Villager 3 Palliasses - to rest your head on.

Laughalot I'm not sure I like the sound of this.

Rainbow It's alright Nanny. Palliasses are just pillows, filled with straw instead of feathers. Come on.

Prince *(looking towards the north)* I wonder?

Villagers and others exit (Dame hesitantly) except the Prince who waits at one side. Rainbow gives a piece of his bread to Trumper on the way out

Enter Jack Frost and his Frosties through the sides, as a little snow falls. Menacing music comes up as the Ice Queen enters through the snow

Jack Frost Oh smashing, we've made it so cold the villagers have run into their homes.

Ice Queen Splendid, and soon we will freeze their doors tight, ha ha. So they will never be able to come out again. Ha ha ha. *(beckons sofly)* Come snow, come.

Snow starts again, and Snowflake and some snowflakes enter, dancing and fluttering around to gentle music

Ice Queen There you are Snowflake. About time too!

Snowflake Oh mother ...

The Prince looks startled

Whilst I like dancing and flurrying in the wind, making pretty swirls with my snowflakes *(indicates them)* everywhere, why must you be so cruel?

Ice Queen CRUEL? CRUEL? All these lands will be mine! And you my daughter dear will grow up to take my place. DO YOU NOT WANT TO CONTROL THE WHOLE WORLD?

Snowflake But mother, you already rule the Northlands, the East and Westlands. Why not leave the people here in peace?

Ice Queen Tell her Jack.

Jack Frost Long ago, as our history is told, we had all the lands. They called it the 'Ice Age'. Our ancestors came and went as they pleased. There were no people, just us; Frosties, Snowflakes, Icicles. It was a time when King Blizzard ruled.

Ice Queen Yes, your great, great, great, great, etc., etc., Grandfather, Snowflake. As you would have remembered, if you had listened when you were a child!

The Prince is listening intently

Jack Frost There were no people to light fires and drive us away. The Sun had little heat, it could not penetrate the snowstorms to melt us. The Moon had no warmth, magic or romance ...

Ice Queen You see my child, why I have hatred, and despise the Sun and Moon?

Snowflake Yes Mother, but ...

Ice Queen No 'buts' daughter dear. What use are you? Oh I wish sometimes that Jack was my son. He understands. He would make a great and magnificent King one day, if only ...

Icicle *(entering)* Hey, super duper. Then we'd get hitched, and I'd be a real co-ol Queen. What say you Jackio baby?

Ice Queen WHAT! The likes of you marrying Jack. Never! You're nothing but an 'Essex' *(or local similar area)* girl! *(then thinking)* Snowflake will marry Jack. Yes! That's it! Why didn't I think of that before? Then they can rule together. Yes. King Jack the first. It sounds wonderful. And as for you, *(looking at Snowflake)* you can flitter flutter as you wish.

Snowflake No mother, I do not want to marry Jack. My heart belongs to ... *(stops herself)*

Ice Queen *(inquisitively)* Yes my child? You were saying *(closing on her)* your heart belongs to WHERE?

Snowflake *(hesitantly)* With, with, with another.

Ice Queen *(menacingly)* Oh yes, and with whom?

Snowflake I, I cannot say.

Ice Queen You will tell me, or I will send you to, to, to, *(lost for words)* to *(local dump area)* Forever!

Snowflake Oh no mother. Not there, please!

Icicle *(doing her nails)* Hey Queenie, stay fresh. Come on Snowflake, tell mumsy about your Princie.

Ice Queen PRINCE! WHAT PRINCE?

Snowflake Oh mother. I only met him yesterday. He's Prince Lionheart, and lives at the Palace in his Kingdom. We fell in love.

Ice Queen WHAT! Jack, isn't that where ...?

Jack Frost Yes Your Majesty, the ...

Ice Queen That Palace is to be mine. From there I shall RULE THE WORLD! Your Prince will suffer and perish with all those foolish people. And you my girl will do as you're told. You WILL marry Jack.

Snowflake is in despair, as is the Prince who is still at the side

Jack Frost *(looking at Snowflake, then Icicle)* Well, I ...

Ice Queen Good. Then there's no more to be said. Come, I haven't fully rested yet, and I must gather my forces for tonight. I will turn my *(looking at Snowflake)* Palace into an ICE PALACE, that will sparkle and glisten until ETERNITY. Ha ...

Menacing music as she says

Blizzards will blow! North winds will howl! Driving sleet will cut through the very souls of mankind! There will be nothing left but vast frozen wastelands! *(sneering laugh)* PURE PARADISE! *(orders)* COME.

They all go to exit. The Prince moves out with arms outstretched (still unseen) as the Ice Queen gets hold of Snowflake and starts to drag her off

When the Palace is won, and the world is conquered, we will prepare for your wedding to Jack. I can see it now *(proudly)* BRIDE OF THE YEAR. All dressed in black. Beautiful, ha ha.

Whilst being dragged out, Snowflake sees Prince. He goes to save her, and she breaks away from her mother. She and the Prince manage to hold hands briefly, outstretched in front, as all others off. But then

Ice Queen Come here Snowflake!

Prince and Snowflake look in despair at each other, break hands. Snowflake off. The Prince goes to follow

Man in Moon *(commands)* STAY PRINCE LIONHEART. Do NOT attempt to save her, yet. She will come to no harm. There is time enough for your feelings. As the Ice Queen said, your Palace is her first target, the 'supposed wedding', later.

Prince *(sadly)* I know, but ... *(blows a kiss after her)*

Man in Moon I fear that there will be new vengeance and determination in the Ice Queen's attack. You should prepare your friends for your journey to Buttercup Meadows. For there is much to be done.

Prince Yes of course. But I knew not that the Ice Queen was Snowflake's mother. She, she is a Princess.

Man in Moon Indeed Your Highness, and, believe me, all will be well. Now, call your friends.

Prince Lottery. Lottery, come hither.

Enter Lottery

Tell the others to make ready We leave shortly for Buttercup Meadows.

Lottery   Rainbow and Nanny, come out of the hay.
            We leave soon. At the break of day.

Rainbow and the Dame emerge, with villagers, children and Trumper. Dame has straw sticking out of her hair, all over the place, and she carries her bag and three others

Rainbow I see the snow has stopped then, yet there's a lot of frost about. Jack Frost and his Frosties I suppose. *(spots Dame and laughs, villagers do likewise)*

Laughalot What's the matter with you lot?

Rainbow Oh nothing. Like your new hair-do. *(sniggers)* Been to ... *(local hairdresser)*

Laughalot What? What are you talking about?

Rainbow *(nonchalantly)* Nothing at all. What are those bags for?

Laughalot As we lost some of our belongings, these are our 'sunny' clothes from the villagers, for when we reach the meadows. They say it will be warm there. *(gives one bag each to Rainbow, Lottery and Prince)* And they said they would give us a picnic, all their last goodies, some of my favourite things. That reminds me of a song.

Song No 9

Dame starts singing, way off key, and with actions as appropriate, wobbles jelly/holds her belly etc., to music of 'A Few Of My Favourite Things')

> Sausage and mash. Ice cream and jelly.
> Large jammy cakes, to fill up my belly.
> A big chocolate gateau covered in cream.
> These are a few things, of which I dream.
> Oho, strawberry tarts, and apple strou-dle.
> Lots of mince pies, covered in ...

All are cringing/covering their ears/howling etc., Lottery goes up to her and puts his hand over her mouth

Prince Well done Lottery.

Man in Moon I will be in bed soon. I see my friend the Sun coming up to the horizon.

Villager 1 *(to Prince)* More food Sire? Some breakfast before we depart?

Prince Thank you. No. I have little appetite at present.

Laughalot Yes please. Always ready for a little bit of something. I would like porridge oats (or large bowl of cornflakes) for breakfast. They always warm me up in winter. How about you Rainbow?

Rainbow No thanks. I prefer a bowl of Frosties. *(starts to scrape the frost (Frosties) into a bowl)*

Prince Enough of this tom foolery.

All look round

What are you looking for?

Rainbow This chap Tom.

Prince Who?

Rainbow Tom Foolery.

Prince It's just a saying. Oh doesn't matter.

Man in Moon I bid you farewell. A safe journey across the Marshlands. The Sun will give you light to see your way. I must sleep soon, for my strengths will be needed later.

Laughalot Oh look, the Sun is rising. That reminds me of another song.

In the wings a bright yellow/orange light starts to come up, and/or a Sun is projected slightly onto the stage

Song No 10

Music starts. Dame sings to 'Aussie' accent, off key, and dances around in a 'stomping' fashion

> Sun arise. He bring in de morning.

Sun arise. He bring in de morning.
Spreading all de light all arounounound.
Sun arise. Oo, Ooo, Sun arise. Oo, Ooo.

Prince Lottery. *(points to Dame)*

Lottery again clamps his hand over her mouth. The others have been covering their ears etc., Dame continues with 'Ooooooo' for a while, whilst the hand is still over her mouth

Man in Moon Thank you Lottery. I could never have slept with that! *(settles down)*

Rainbow Mind you Your Highness, we should sing a song to keep us happy whilst we travel.

Prince Oh. I know not. We are tired and cold. The Ice Queen has frozen the lands and now she is after my Palace. We don't know the secret. We have now to cross these murky frozen marshes, AND, she intends to marry off to someone else the one I love!

Rainbow 'Tis not like you Sire to be miserable. This not an audition for 'Eastenders' *(pause)* What say you Lottery?

Lottery   Well it does appear much trouble and strife,
But always look on the bright side of life.

Lottery points to yellow light which is getting brighter, or Sun now rising

Prince You are right. I must be courageous, and bring the happiness back to my people.

Song No 11

All sing, 'Always Look On The Bright Side Of Life' or 'Happy Wanderer'. The four travellers move to front of stage, with villagers behind. As 'Bright Side Of Life' is sung they sweep/point to the Sun/bright orange light. The song has a natural tempo, and a 'four step' dance like the 'Shadows' used is very effective. Or, a backward/forward stepping movement with arms swinging, by the front four, and swaying (positive action to the beat) by villagers is quite acceptable.

The song ends if possible with arms outstretched high to the front, or towards the rising Sun, with voices on a high note, to give a rousing, exciting finish to the First Act. An alternative ending is for Lottery to say,

We must go forward. Courage will not lack.
Journey westwards, with knapsacks on our back.

He indicates the bags/knapsacks Nanny has given them. Then all sing, 'The Happy Wanderer'

Curtains down on Act 1

INTERVAL

During the interval, it is suggested that, on a Saturday night, immediately the curtains are drawn on Act 1, Lottery is given the winning lottery numbers, and emerges through the curtains to say;

> Ladies and gentlemen, I have news good and true.
> And if the Lottery you win, the drinks are on you.
> The numbers this week are a bit of a mix.**
> They are A, B, C, D, E, and number six.
> Number z is the bonus number to boot.
> I hope that you all win lots of loot.

** A slip of paper can be prepared beforehand with the appropriate message. If there is no number ending in six, then the following alternatives are suggested

> The numbers this week will give you more and more - four.
> The numbers this week, so lucky may be - three.
> The numbers this week are no doubt for you - two.
> The numbers this week are both yours and mine - nine. etc., etc.,

ACT 2

Scene 1

Buttercup Meadows. A sunny meadow with appropriate background of trees and lowish hills in distance. This scene (full stage) should contain a striking effect of yellows, oranges and reds, where possible and a minimum of green foliage. Lighting should be bright yellowish. The Sun is bright on the backcloth with a yellowish hue to the blue sky. The Moon is faintly outlined (whitish) in same position as in Act 1. There is a Tollgate stile to the left. The Tollkeeper (wearing bright yellow boots) is in front of it

Villagers and children are picking buttercups/flowers, and as music starts, form positions to dance. Adults at the back in two rows, juveniles at the front

Song No 12

All sing, 'Oh What A Beautiful Morning'. As they start singing, the adults sway to the music, with arms out, swinging from side to side. Juveniles are holding hands, and also swaying initially, then they interweave, sort of skipping, through the adults, as the adults half skip/step towards the front, and then back again. The juveniles ending up in front of the adults at the end of the dance. All have arms outstretched as the song ends on a high note. As the song fades, some of the villagers move to the sides, and other villagers say, 'Come on children, let's go for a walk in the meadow'. Some of the children go off, ready for costume change to create the rainbow (if necessary). The Tollkeeper takes up his position by the stile

Rainbow *(entering in bright sunny waistcoat)* Hi everyone!
Audience HI RAINBOW!
Tollkeeper That will be 2p please.
Rainbow I haven't got 2p, they haven't been invented yet. How about a groat?
Tollkeeper I'm sorry. 2p or you can't come into the meadow. Lot of upkeep and costs you know. *(to audience)* And I need a refreshing mug of ale later. All this hard work.
Rainbow What hard work?
Tollkeeper Getting money out of people like you. Come on 2p or no entry.
Rainbow *(brightly)* OK, right. Time for some magic. ABRACADABULOUS! *(swirls his cape, wobbles his wand and a large 2p is produced, with a large hole in it, but covered with brown paper as if whole)*
Tollkeeper *(amazed)* I can't accept that, it's far too big. I won't get it into my pouch.
Rainbow *(looks at Tollkeeper)* Well you can wear it! *(smashes it over his head, to crash on cymbals, looks round)* Ah here comes Dame Laughalot.

Enter Dame Laughalot in 'sunny' outfit loaded up with a blanket, picnic box, food hanging from her pockets, including a string of sausages, and her bag

Laughalot Oh dear, this is so heavy. *(brightly)* We had to bring the picnic along to this lovely meadow. The villagers emptied their stores, lock, stock, but sadly no barrel. They said that as the Prince was going to destroy the Ice Queen, we might as well have a feast.
Tollkeeper That will be 2p please madam.
Laughalot What for?
Tollkeeper Entry to the meadow madam.
Laughalot How do you expect me to give you 2p when I'm carrying all this lot?
Tollkeeper Sorry madam, you can't come in unless you give me 2p.
Laughalot Well hold this lot then!

She starts to unload all her picnic effects onto Tollkeeper, who places them on the other of the stile, but retains a basket. Then, in a most unlady-like manner, showing her bloomers, she climbs over the stile. When she gets to the other side, she pulls out of her pocket a largish 2p, attached to a piece of string. She takes basket from Tollkeeper, and gives him the 2p. As Tollkeeper goes to put it in his pouch, the Dame pulls it back, and does her silly laugh. The Dame then starts to pick up her things, she drops one, picks up another, her bonnet falls off etc., to create a hilarious comedy sketch during which her knickers fall down

Audience KNICKERS!

Eventually she is nearly there, with sausages under her bonnet. She sees Rainbow, who has been bemused by the situation. Dame collapses in a heap

Laughalot Well don't just stand there, give me a hand.
Rainbow *(thinking)* Time again for some magic I believe. One, two, three -
ABRACADABULOUS! *(swirls his cape and wobbles his wand - a large hand
is produced, either a kitchen glove blown up, or a largish cardboard/made-up
one)* Here you are Nanny. *(laughing, throws it to her)*
Laughalot That's no good. You must be off your trolley!
Rainbow Ah, of course. ABRACADABULOUS! *(by the side, he swirls his cape
and wobbles his wand and a supermarket trolley is pushed on stage)*
Laughalot *(sweetly)* Oh thank you Rainbow. You are wonderful.

*They start loading the trolley as the Prince enters in 'sunny' outfit. Dame
watches as the Tollkeeper touches his forelock, bows, and helps the Prince
over the stile, although of course the Prince can manage quite confidently*

Prince Oh what a beautiful morning.
Laughalot They've just sung that. They're not going to sing it again. *(to Tollkeeper)*
How come he doesn't have to pay?
Tollkeeper He's in the National Trust.
Laughalot Huh! *(goes to the far right of stage, hitching up her knickers, and
starts to unload the trolley/lay the picnic on the blanket)*

Enter Villager 1 with Trumper, who is holding in his paws a pair of scissors

Song No 13

Music starts. Villager 1 is singing, 'One Man Went To Mow'

> One man went to mow, went to mow a meadow.
> One man and his dog, went to mow a meadow.

When he stops, the Tollkeeper looks at them amazed

Tollkeeper It will take you years to cut the meadow with those!
Villager 1 I'm not, the dog is.
Tollkeeper What! Talk about leading a dog's life. *(officially)* Anyway, 2p to
come in.

Villager searches himself, pulls out his pockets, - nothing - shrugs shoulders

Tuu, pee, please sir.
Villager 1 Oh, tuu, pee.

*Takes off wig to reveal a bald head. Gives wig to Tollkeeper who looks weirdly
at wig and Villager's baldness*

Don't look at me like that. I'll have you know this is a bald wig! *(points to
head)*

Tollkeeper shakes his head and puts the wig in his pouch, as Villager and Trumper go into meadow. Villager sits down at side. Trumper starts to cut the grass, fussed over by others. Then Lottery enters in 'sunny' outfit

Tollkeeper 2p please sir.
Lottery The good news or the bad news?
Tollkeeper The bad news.
Lottery   You ask an impossible request of me,
            For I have never owned - a 2p.
Tollkeeper Well what's the good news?
Lottery   Have one of my tickets instead, my good friend.
            For it may bring luck before this Panto does end.
            (gives Tollkeeper a Lottery ticket)
Tollkeeper *(looking at it)* Let's hope it does, kind sir. *(kisses it, turns round three times to the amusement of the others)*

A large finger on the end of a long pole comes out of the sky, and points at Tollkeeper. A deep voice, from offstage, then says, 'It could be you'. All react/ gasps/awe etc.,

Prince Well everyone, we are in the meadow. How are we for time?
Villager 1 'Tis nearly midday Your Highness.
Prince Thank you good sir. *(looks round)* There's no sign of a rainbow though.
Rainbow *(being a bit silly)* That's because the Sun is shining, but there isn't any rain. You need both for a rainbow to appear.
Laughalot *(still spreading out her picnic on one side, now assisted by the villagers and children, as Trumper is sniffing around)* Everyone knows that. Why don't you grow up. Stupid!
Rainbow *(even more silly)* I did grow up stupid! He he.
Laughalot *(sitting on her blanket and looking around)* Oh look, there's the Man in the Moon, sleeping, whilst we're down here doing everything to save the Kingdom, and the whole world, from that wicked Ice Queen. Working hard, facing all kinds of danger. No time to rest, starving *(goes to take a big bite from a cake)* Oh look, *(sarcastically)* so peaceful and quiet.

Man in the Moon has been snoring gently. He now emits a big snore

Oh shut up! *(throws the string of sausages at him)*

The sausages are retrieved by Trumper. Dame then takes a bite from the cake in a very unlady-like manner

Prince Well, we need some rain now.
Laughalot *(spluttering on her cake)* Not until I've finished my picnic we don't.
Prince *(ignoring Dame)* Rainbow, this is where you come in.
Rainbow But I am in. Paid my 2p I did.
Prince *(laughing)* I know that. I meant, this is where you come in.
Rainbow *(confused)* I am in. *(to audience)* Am I not in?

Audience YES!

Rainbow *(to audience)* You saw me pay my 2p didn't you?

Audience YES!

Prince *(still laughing, goes to Rainbow and puts arm around his shoulder)* I know you are in. What I mean, this is where you come in with your magic.

Rainbow Oh, right. I see now. I like making magic, but making rain is very difficult. *(thinks)* I know, I'll make a Rainmaker. I need help to conjure up people. *(to audience)* Will you help, please?

Audience Yes!

Rainbow You'll have to help me say the magic word - ABRACADABULOUS. Is that OK?

Audience Yes!

Rainbow Right. A little practise with me, after three, ready, one, two, three - ABRACADABULOUS.

Audience ABRACADABULOUS!

Rainbow Splendid. Got it first time. Well done, but a little louder when I do my magic - alright?

Audience Yes!

Rainbow *(moving to Tollkeeper, who is standing by the wings, and gets out his wobbly wand, and swirls his cape over the Tollkeeper)* Ready, one, two, three - ABRACADABULOUS!

Underneath the cape Tollkeeper sheds his velcroed Tollkeeper outfit to reveal bright yellow 'sowesters' with yellow hat. Throws off old clothes to wings. Retains his bright yellow boots. If the process does not work too well or is a bit slow, or on the other occasions later, then Rainbow should make a joke of it with, 'Oh my magic is failing again', quietly, but for the audience to hear, then louder, 'Come on, get a move on, speed it up a bit. Ah my magic is at last working'. Rainbow must try to keep his cape swirled over the person and keep his back to the audience. He can turn his head when speaking, if appropriate

Tollkeeper/Rainmaker *(looking round)* Ah, it must be the weekend again!

Prince Well done Rainbow. *(to audience)* and all. Now Rainmaker, we need your help. The secret of how to stop the Ice Queen is at the end of the rainbow. So we need some rain.

Rainmaker Well, I only normally work at weekends, but if it's to help stop the Ice Queen, then ...

Laughalot *(breaking into song)* 'Just one cornetto ...'

Rainmaker I said Ice Queen, not ice cream!

Laughalot Oh I thought you said ice cream.

Prince I don't think that anyone, least of all you, could confuse the Ice Queen with ice cream.

Laughalot Anyway I thought he said ice cream. I want some to go with my jelly. *(pulls out a jelly on a plate and sings)* Wibble wobbie, wibble wobble. Jelly on a plate. *(to audience)* I bet you'd like to see my jellies wobble, wouldn't you? Well you can't. I didn't show you my 'wobbles' earlier, and you're not going to see my 'jellies' now. I'm going to finish the rest of my picnic, then you may be in for a treat. Ah ha ha. *(sits with side to audience, and back to Rainmaker)*

Rainmaker Just a little rain *(pulls out a small watering-can with a sprinkler, walks over to Dame, and pours a few drops over her. The blanket should absorb the water)*

Laughalot Ah, oh it's only a drop of rain, must finish the picnic before it starts to pour.

Rainmaker pours on a little more

Oh well, who cares! *(sings)*
> It's raining it's pouring.
> The Man in the Moon is snoring.
> He stays up all night, shining so bright.
> And goes to sleep in the morning.

Rainmaker This will dampen her appetite. *(goes to empty can over Dame who notices in time. Lets a little go over her, or a lot if you so wish)*

Laughalot *(getting and approaching him, looking him up and down)* Haven't I seen you somewhere before? You remind me of the man.

Rainmaker What man?

Laughalot The man at the stile.

Rainmaker What stile?

Laughalot Well you certainly haven't got any (style). *(laughs outrageously and nudges him in side with her elbow, sending him flying)* Style. No style. Ha ha. *(sees audience is not laughing, goes to front to explain)* Style! You know, clothes, dress sense, like what I've got. Funneee, no? Well, suit yourselves. Ha ha, joke, style, suit yourselves, suit. Oh I give up! Oh is that you out there Mrs .... *(local dignitary/friend in audience)* Lottery told me you're going on holiday. Take heed of what Confucius say. He say, *(Chinese accent)* 'Suntanned lady like well cooked chicken - white bits are the tastiest!' Ah ha ha. *(goes back to picnic)*

Prince *(looking around disheartened)* Lottery, whilst we are trying to get some rain, go forth to the north, to see what the Ice Queen is up to.

Lottery   Off I go to the land of the snow,
> Where all about is freezing.
> I wish I didn't have to go,
> I'll only end up sneezing.

Prince We'll make sure you get a warm welcome on your return.

Lottery exits

Now come on Rainmaker. Bring us rain, with haste.

Rainmaker Are you ready?

Song No 14

Music starts. Rainmaker sings,

> Bring me sunshine. Bring me rain.
> Bring me lots of it. Make it pour again.
> Sunrays come from the Sun, and raindrops from the sky.

Bring me sunshine, bring me rain.
Bring me ra.....in!

He dances across the stage, as per 'Morecambe and Wise'. One hand hitting behind the head, the other hitting the foot up behind him. Swapping alternate steps. Everyone stands to the sides, as the Rainmaker stops. And as the new music starts, all on stage sing the song as Sunrays and Raindrops enter from wings, mingling and dancing together

Song No 15

'Sing A Rainbow'. As all sing, enter seven (or fourteen, see costume notes) juveniles, each dressed as a colour of the rainbow (in colour order, with a brief pause between each one) This can be a beautiful dance. Scene ends with a rainbow, just off centre stage, the juveniles next to each other and leaning over in an arc, arms outstretched over head/in front. (if fourteen they can touch)

An alternative suggestion, coloured cardboard/plywood can be used for the rainbow. This is recommended for small sized productions. See Stage Notes for concept, together with ideas for similar dance routines. At the end of the song

Laughalot Beautiful, oh so beautiful, though it does look a bit like a 'Dulux' advert! *(stands up watching, hitching up her knickers)*

Prince Well done Rainmaker, and Rainbow of course. Now hurry we must get to the end of the rainbow to find the secret. *(advances towards rainbow, but it moves away. Stops, and the rainbow stops. Moves forward again, and rainbow does likewise. Stops again, and rainbow stops, just by wings/base of Man in the Moon's platform, see stage notes)* Of course, the rainbow always moves away. How are we going to get to the end?

Rainbow Even my magic can't help here.

Laughalot Oh well, it's time to go home to a horrible cold house. *(starts packing up picnic, looks at watch)* What's the time? *(shakes it)* Oh it's stopped, it must have got wet in the rain.

Rainbow *(excited)* Oh you are clever Dame Laughalot. That's the answer.

Laughalot Who, me? *(laughs)* Oh I am a clever one. *(confused)* What answer?

Rainbow To stop time. If only we can stop time somehow, we can get to the end of the rainbow.

Prince Brilliant Rainbow. Use your magic again.

Rainbow I'm afraid Sire, my magic is not powerful enough to stop time. *(to everyone)* BUT I KNOW A MAN WHO CAN!

Prince Who?

Rainbow The Man in the Moon. He is so magical he can do anything.

Enter Lottery

Prince Ah Lottery. What news of the wicked Ice Queen?

Lottery The good news or the bad news Sire?

Prince The bad news.

Lottery I went forth, to the north.
      Beyond the Watford Junction. *
      To a land so white and oh so cold,
      My mind it would not function. * *(* amend as appropriate)*

Prince Come on Lottery old chap, what's the good news?

Lottery The Ice Queen, she sleeps today.
      And the Sun is shiny and bright.
      It is a time to dance and play.
      But the Queen, she attacks early tonight.

Prince Well we have some respite, but really there's no time to lose.

Laughalot *(laughing)* Yes there is.

Prince Oh yes. Come on Rainbow, you said the Man in the Moon could help. OF COURSE, he said earlier, that, 'TIME STANDETH STILL FOR NO MAN'. He is the MOON. He's been here since the beginning of time itself, thus he is part of time. He just has to stop himself.

Rainbow Yes, and we'll need special magic to reach him during the day, unless of course he wakes up for his midday snack.

Laughalot Midday snack. What are you talking about?

Rainbow Well you have a midnight snack sometimes, don't you?

Laughalot Yes, last night I had three jam sandwiches, eight sausage rolls, then a chocolate and cream gateau, followed by spotted dick and custard, and three cups of tea, and then ... *(knickers fall down)*

Audience ~~KNICKERS!~~

Prince *(aghast)* What!

Laughalot *(hoisting up knickers, to audience)* ~~Thank you.~~ *(to Prince)* That was for starters, and then ...

Prince Oh, I see. Enough of this. Rainbow, can you wake the Man in the Moon?

Rainbow Well he did give me a secret word, only to be used in an emergency though.

Prince Well this is an emergency.

Rainbow We'll have to say it very loud.

All We will.

Rainbow *(to audience)* Will you help too?

Audience YES!

Laughalot Well, what is this magic word?

Rainbow The Man in the Moon said it's a secret. I can't tell you.

Laughalot Don't be silly. You've got to tell us if we have to shout it out loud.

Rainbow No. Not telling. *(to audience)* You can't tell secrets, can you?

Audience NO!

Rainbow See. Told you.

Laughalot Told me what?

Prince If you don't want to say the secret word, mime it, quickly now, and we'll guess it.

Laughalot Oh yes. I love charades. I'm ever so good at it.

Rainbow Right then. *(thinking painfully)* Here goes. *(goes into a throwing of arms/jumps/twirls etc.,)*

Laughalot Oh, that's simple. it's - *(dancing, to music, if desired)* SUPERCALIFRAGILISTICEXPEALIDOCIOUS.

Song.

Everyone is amazed, except Rainbow

Rainbow I must have done the mime too easy.
Prince Is that really it Rainbow?
Rainbow Yes - SUPERCALIFRAGILISTICEXPEALIDOCIOUS.
Prince Right everybody, one, two, three ...
All/audience SUPERCALIFRAGILISTICEXPEALIDOCIOUS.

Slight movement from the Man in the Moon

Rainbow *(to audience)* Not loud enough - again ...
All/audience SUPERCALIFRAGILISTICEXPEALIDOCIOUS.

Man in the Moon snuffles/snorts and wakes up

Man in Moon What? Who calls? Who wakens me in the middle of the day?
Rainbow We did Man in the Moon.
Prince Please, we would like to stop time, just long enough for us to reach the
end of the rainbow, to find the secret.
Man in Moon You did well Your Highness, to remember my words, and Rainbow
did well to remember the secret of how to awaken me.
Laughalot Huh! I guessed it.
Man in Moon Really. You are indeed a gifted one.
Laughalot I know. I know. *(curtseys all round, laughs and smiles at her 'fans')*
Man in Moon Ah, you have a wonderful rainbow.
Prince Yes but it won't last long, and we can't reach the end, unless you stop
time for us. Then we can get the secret of how to stop the Ice Queen. Be rid of
her forever.
Man in Moon Your Highness, you have learnt well, but not well enough, yet.
Prince I don't understand.
Man in Moon You will Sire, you will. Now, are you ready to dig for the secret?
Rainbow No, but won't be a moment. Hm, we need a gardener. One, two, three
... ABRACADABULOUS.

*Gets out his wobbly wand, and swirls his cape around the Rainmaker who is
on one side. Rainmaker, under cover of the cape, takes off his hat and sowesters,
and throws them off stage. The watering can falls to the side, still on stage, to
reveal a gardener, still wearing the bright yellow boots. Also, a sign around his
neck for all to see, 'DINERS - DIG FOR VICTORY - ON CREDIT'*

Rainbow Will that do?
Laughalot *(laughing)* Oh, what a card. 'That'll do nicely'.
Lottery   Your Highness, and Man in the Moon,
                   We must stop time now, for it is noon.

All look up at the Man in the Moon

Man in Moon   OH GOD OF HEAVEN, AND ALL ABOVE,

LISTEN TO MY PLEA OF WARMTH AND LOVE.
LIGHT MUST FLASH AS FASTER WE GO,
ON THROUGH TIME AND SPACE WE FLOW,
FASTER AND FASTER WE TRAVEL UNTIL,
WE CATCH UP LIGHT, AND TIME STANDS STILL.

As he speaks in booming voice, music, roll of drums, and lights begin to flash gently, then into strobe lighting, if possible, also switch on Ultra Violet lighting, and 'explode' a pyrotechnic - to indicate, 'Time Standing Still'. If no pyrotechnic available, a single clash of cymbals can give a good effect. Players now move and speak in a slowish motion, as the Man in the Moon stands 'powerfully' looking to the heavens with arms outstretched. Fog or mist, if possible

(slowly) All is now stopped, you can proceed. You have a few moments *(to audience)* relatively speaking of course. This moment in history will give Professor Einstein something to think about!

All move slowly to the end of the rainbow, which remains where it is. They all crowd round as the gardener digs slowly, and unearths (from wings, or under a sort of tunnel effect protruding from the wings/part of landscape/or under the moon) a golden pot containing white crystals, a Dish and Spoon (juveniles) Prudence, (with fiddle) Smelly and Rudolph. All are as if 'frozen solid'. Also a Cadbury's Cream Easter Egg, not seen by audience, and an old coin

Man in Moon *(slowly)* My power is fading, complete your task.

Music slows, then explode a pyrotechnic, or cymbal crash, and switch off Ultra Violet and Strobe Lighting. All back to normal, although Man in the Moon looks exhausted. As the event closes, the rainbow moves off stage

Prince See, the rainbow has gone. We must be back to normal time.
Rainbow Who am I? Where am I? What happened?
Laughalot You are Rainbow. We are in Buttercup Meadows. And what happened? That's easy. Basically, as you approach the speed of light, time slows down in relation to other objects. For example, if you run across the meadow, it wouldn't take you as long as an ant who is only crawling along. If you ran at the speed of light - 299,792.5 kilometres a second, or 186,282.4 miles per second, you would be with light itself, thus you'd be across the meadow in NO time. See, no time is to stop time. Easy, isn't it? *(pondering)* he must have done that by gravity. *(all are standing absolutely dumbfounded as she speaks. Then quite nonchalantly goes to the pile of objects)* Now, what have we here?

The others come over, scratching their heads in bewilderment at Dame's speech. They look at the pile

Man in Moon *(recovered)* You see Your Highness what a knowledgeable Nanny you have.

Prince looks at her and nods, slowly, as if thinking to Man in the Moon

Rainbow You are clever Nanny.
Laughalot Oh I know. *(digs him in the ribs with elbow, and sort of silly)* I know! *(bends down and picks up Roman coin)* This is just an old coin.
Gardener Treasure trove. I'll have that. *(takes it)*
Man in Moon And I'll have those. *(points to his pets, Dish and Spoon)* I wondered where that Ice Queen had hidden them.
Rainbow *(exclaims)* And look! I'll have that. *(grabs the Easter egg, still hidden from the audience, his back to them, clutches it in hand)*
Laughalot No. I want it. *(goes to take it)*
Rainbow No, you can't have it. I saw it first. It's mine. It must be mine, look at all those bright colours.
All *(except Prince)* No, I/we want it.

A struggle ensues with everyone trying to take the egg from Rainbow. He breaks free. Also villager and children who went for the 'meadow walk' can now reappear on stage

Rainbow It's so rare. There's not another anywhere. It's priceless. It's unique. AND IT'S MINE!
Prince STOP! *(all stop fighting)* Rainbow, come here. What is it that everyone appears to want? Is it the secret?
Rainbow *(going to Prince reluctantly)* No You Highness, it's ...
Lottery *(interrupting)*
                              'Tis of no importance. The secret it is not.
                              For that is contained in the golden pot.
                              What Rainbow has is good, I do declare,
                              But soon those things - will be everywhere.
                              (wide sweeping gestures)
Prince Well show us. Oh no ...

Rainbow slowly holds up the Cream Egg for all/audience to see. Prince looks, shakes his head, then wanders over to the pot. If the audience is large, and it is a long way to the back, the Prince can exclaim, 'A Cadbury's Cream Easter Egg'.

Laughalot There's nothing for me, boo ho. *(hitches up knickers)*
Rainbow You can have these. They'll come in useful to you. *(points to dish and spoon)*

Gardener moves to pick them up and give to her. Dame approaches him

Laughalot Just a minute. *(looks him up and down)* Haven't I seen you somewhere before? Yellow Wellington boots. You remind me of the Man.
Gardener What Man?
Laughalot The Man with the watering can.
Gardener What watering can?

Laughalot This one. *(picks it up and starts hitting him with it)* Make me all wet would you. Take that, and that. That'll teach you to wet my bonnet!

Gardener Hey, hang on a minute. How's about I wet your whistle down at *(local pub)* later, and we can have a little chat, just you and me? I think you've had a bit too much Sun, and ...

They go into a huddle and start chatting. The Dame is warming to the idea of a drink, and to the Gardener

Prince This secret. What can it be? *(holding the golden pot)*

Rainbow A moment Your Highness. See, the animals are stirring.

The pets all start to awaken from their frozen slumber, a little shivering, then basking in the Sun

Look Man in the Moon, your cat, your dog, and your cow.

Man in Moon *(beaming)* I can see. Oh how happy I am. Look, see how my friend the Sun is warming them.

Prince This is wonderful! *(then melancholy)* How I wish my Snowflake was here, to share in our happiness. To share this magic moment.

Man in Moon With my pets returned safe and well, my happiness and power are returning. Magic moments will be yours, Your Highness, and Snowflake will be invisible to ALL, except you and me.

Song No 16

The others make a fuss of the pets, oblivious to anything, as the music 'Magic Moments' or 'Love Changes Everything' starts, and Snowflake enters, with Icicle, who sits down with her headphones on, listening to other music

Prince Is this really you, Snowflake?

Snowflake Oh Prince Lionheart. I knew you would find a way.

They hold hands and sing   Song 16

Icicle *(as song fades)* Hey Snowflake, you finished yet with Princie? This place is giving me the 'Hots'. We had better move it, back to the 'co - ol' lands.

Snowflake Farewell my Prince. Please bring us together again soon.

Prince *(sadly)* Farewell my Snowflake. *(confidently)* Somehow, I will find a way for us to be together.

Snowflake and Icicle exit. Prince blows her a kiss

Rainbow Man in the Moon, your cat, and your dog, and your cow are longing to see you.

Prudence Meo - ow.

Smelly Woof. Woof.

Rudolf Moo. Mooooooo.

Man in Moon Ah, look. They have missed me as much as I have missed them. Pass up Prudence so I may stroke her.

Villagers and/or Lottery lift up Prudence, who, if possible, sits on Man in Moon's lap, and purrs loudly. If not possible, then lift up to be stroked and return to floor

Oh Prudence, how pretty and soft you are. Now let me see Smelly.

Villagers back away a bit

He's not really smelly you know. *(laughing)*

Villagers pass up Smelly. Man in Moon tickles him under the chin and pats him. Smelly 'woofs' a little and is returned to the floor

Rainbow I think we'll all have to help up Rudolf. Why do you call him Rudolph, Man in the Moon?

Villagers, Dame, Rainbow and Lottery all try to lift the cow

Man in Moon *(laughing)* Santa gave him to me at Christmas. Quite apt don't you think?

They are all trying very hard to lift the cow, but fail

Lottery   *(to Man in the Moon)*
                  I think that now is perhaps the time,
                  To recite your favourite nursery rhyme.
Man in Moon Why yes indeed young Lottery. What a good idea. *(to audience)* Oh I am so happy. Will you say my nursery rhyme with me please?
Audience YES!
Man in Moon Do you all know it? It goes, *(music if desired)* 'HEY DIDDLE DIDDLE - THE CAT AND THE FIDDLE'. Let's all say it together. Ready,
All/audience *(music again, if desired)* HEY DIDDLE DIDDLE, THE CAT AND THE FIDDLE. THE COW JUMPED OVER THE MOON ...

Note: *This next sequence should be quite slick where appropriate, and can be very funny. The cow attempts to jump over the moon, but falls on top of Dame Laughalot. They both end up on the floor*

Laughalot *(as they are being helped up)* Get off me, you silly old cow!
Rudolph Who are you calling a silly old cow? Old cow yourself! *(starts to butt Dame with her horns)*
Laughalot You, you overweight piece of beef.
Rudolph Huh. You're just a piece of mutton dressed as lamb.
Laughalot Well - Baaaaaaa to you!

Rudolph pushes Dame round the stage. Dame hitches up her knickers to amusement/concern of the others

Laughalot I'll have you know I'm only 21 years old!

Rudolph Pull the 'Udder One'. *(lifts leg)* Anyway I'm only three and a half million years young, so watch it.

Laughalot *(optional)* Oh Bullocks. *(to audience)* I said Bullocks!

Prince Oh Nanny, go and wash your mouth out with soap and water.

Laughalot *(to Rudolph)* Let me show you how to do it. *(knickers fall down)*

Audience KNICKERS!

Laughalot *(hoists up knickers - to audience)* I must get some new elastic when I get home. *(quite unlady-like takes a sort of 'get ready', then does a sort of 'leap' over the moon, failing miserably, falling in a heap, to drumroll or cymbal crash)*

Rainbow Well, you can't call that *(American accent)* One small step for man - one giant leap for mankind!

Man in Moon *(laughing)* Stop! Stop! Enough. Let's try again. *(to audience and all)* Ready everyone? Yes. Good. Here goes then ...

All/audience *(music?)* HEY DIDDLE DIDDLE - THE CAT AND THE FIDDLE. *(cat plays the fiddle)* THE COW JUMPED OVER THE MOON. *(cow leaps with help of two/three villagers/rope, up to/over the moon)* THE LITTLE DOG LAUGHED TO SEE SUCH FUN. *(Smelly rolls on his back and laughs/barks, whilst waving his paws in the air)* AND THE DISH RAN AWAY WITH THE SPOON. *(Dish and Spoon run round the stage, then off through audience)*

Man in Moon Oh, my Dish and Spoon. Do your business Smelly.

Smelly goes to Dame Laughalot, and from a 'squeezy' bottle hidden inside costume, squeezes some water as if from hind leg which is raised

Laughalot Ahhh - get away you naughty beast!

Man in Moon *(laughing)* No Smelly, not your business. I meant go and fetch my Dish and Spoon.

Smelly looks up at Man in Moon, then from front of stage out into the audience. He then runs off into the audience, followed by Trumper, the villager's dog

Prince Oh such fun. But I think we have forgotten why we are here.

Rainbow *(composing himself)* Yes indeed Sire. Let us collect the secret, and back to the Palace for nightfall when the wicked Ice Queen cometh.

Man in Moon Yes Prince. The secret is in the golden pot. Make haste, and please look after my pets, for the time being, until we have accomplished our task.

Cat is taken from Man in Moon, if appropriate. Villagers take cat and cow

Man in Moon Where's Smelly? He hasn't come back yet. I can't lose him again. Please find him.

Dame, Rainbow and a couple of Villagers go into audience, shouting and looking round. House lights or spotlights up

Laughalot Smelly, where are you, you naughty dog. Smelly. Smelly, no not you sir. I didn't call you Smelly. Trumper, no not you madam etc.,

Rainbow Smelly. Smelly, here boy, look, I've conjured up a bone for you. *(magics up a bone)*

Villagers Smelly. Trumper. Come here, there's good doggies etc.,

Smelly and Trumper are at the back of the audience, with the Dish and the Spoon, and all return to the stage. Dish and Spoon chased by villagers. Smelly and Trumper carried to, and 'dumped' on stage. Carriers move to their places as if nothing had happened. Two dogs look at each other and whine a little, then slink off and find the sausages, getting one end each. Prince and Lottery laugh at the antics, then inspect the golden pot

Man in Moon Thank you my good friends. I shall now go back to sleep for a while. I, no, we will have a hard night ahead.

Prince Before you settle down Man in the Moon, I do not understand this, this secret. These white crystals. *(holds up the golden pot)*

Man in Moon Think long and hard of its CONTENT - THINK OF THE SNOW COVERED FROZEN LANDS, AND THE TURBULENT ICE FREE SEAS. THINK ALSO OF YOUR CHILDHOOD. BUT MOST OF ALL THINK WISELY, FOR THE SECRET OF HOW TO STOP THE ICE QUEEN WILL BE REVEALED ONLY TO YOU. IT IS IN YOUR HANDS, AND WITHIN YOU YOURSELF.

Villagers You must destroy the Ice Queen/kill her/and save us etc.,

Man in Moon Heed well what I have said Your Highness. I know you will do what is good and right.

Prince *(pondering)* I will. I will.

Man in Moon Goodnight, nay, Good-day Your Highness, and all you good people. And be good Rudolph, Prudence, and most of all you Smelly.

Smelly and Trumper are pulling with their teeth at each end of the string of sausages, both wanting them. They tug and tug, growling, and end up near front of stage. Everyone is laughing. Dame gets pair of scissors used by Trumper to cut grass, goes to them, and cuts middle. Dogs fall apart, and, howling, roll over backwards to each side. Dame puts scissors away

Laughalot Share and share alike. That's right isn't it everyone?

All *(laughing)* Yes of course Nanny/Dame Laughalot.

Man in Moon *(laughing)* No more. No more. Safe journey home. I will see you all tonight. *(settles down and goes to sleep)*

Laughalot Right then, come on everybody. Let's get home to a nice cup of tea. You can't beat a good cup of tea after a long day, lovely.

All get ready, picnic things packed up into trolley etc.,

Rainbow Have you got the secret Your Highness of how to destroy that nasty terrible Ice Queen?

Prince It appears I have, though I haven't discovered yet how it will work.

Villager 1 But you must destroy the Ice Queen, Your Highness.

Villager 2 We have no food left now. *(looks at Dame who reacts as if, 'who me')*
Villager 3 The Ice Queen is going to freeze us all tonight.
Villager 4 And your kingdom!
Villager 5 And your Palace.
Prince Well, as Nanny says, let's get back as quick as we can. I will have to work out what to do on the way back, and I will speak to the Man in the Moon later. Are we all ready, and the pets?
All Yes.
Laughalot I've had a lovely day, the Sun, the rainbow, the picnic, the meadows, the flowers. *(picks big daisy)* A lovely day out.
Rainbow Me too. All that magic, and as for that 'stopping time' business, what excitement! *(to villagers)* And don't worry now, the Man in the Moon and our Prince will save us all.

Villagers look happier

Prince *(happily)* I have the secret, and I have seen my love again. *(confident)* I now have something to fight for, for Snowflake will be MY bride.
Laughalot And if we go back now those nasty little Mibbie Mibbies won't get us. They won't be out until tonight.

All are now happy and confident

Prince Well come, let's go. *(confident, pointing homeward)* Lottery, to the fore, through the Murky Marshes and the Black Forest.

Song No 17

Music starts. They start a sort of march

Lottery   Here we go again, happy as can be.
                   All good pals and jolly good company.

All sing, 'Here We Go Again'. A dance routine continues until the end. After an initial sort of march, the dance can turn into a very jovial demonstrative one, with twirls and weaving in and out

Prince *(as music fades)* Homeward - to the Palace!

All wave and start to move off. Curtain

Scene 2

On the journey home. Front of tabs. Enter Dame Laughalot carrying the daisy from the meadow, and bag containing her bottles, about six tickle sticks/feather dusters, and the same number of Cadbury's Cream eggs

Laughalot I think Rainbow's gone off me. I wonder if he has. *(takes off petals)* He loves me, he loves me not. He loves me... *(end on a 'not')* He loves me not. *(sadly)* I thought so. Don't want to live without him. Think I'll kill myself. I suppose I could jump from here. *(to front, looks over)* Oh no, can't stand heights. Anyway I might fall on you and flatten you and spread blood everywhere. You wouldn't want that, would you? Oh, you would would you? Well here goes. No, it might hurt. I think I'll have a drink to cheer me up. *(pulls out empty sherry bottle)* Oh no, empty. Things getting worse. I'll have to kill myself. I know, pills. *(takes out pill bottle, reads label)* Take one, three times a day. That's a slow death isn't it? How about if I drown myself? *(takes out Hottie Bottie)* Not enough water here. I could try and eat myself to death, although I was on a diet last week, lost three inches off my waist. *(to member of audience)* Oh Mrs *(local dignitary/friend)* I see you found them, and put them on. Ah well, I suppose I'll just have to laugh it off. *(exclaims)* THAT'S IT! My name, Dame Laughalot. I'll laugh myself to death. Can you make faces at me? Ha, that's a funny one. Sorry, you haven't started yet. Come on please, lots of funny faces. Oh that's good. More please. *(laughs more earnestly, then stops)* No good, I'm still alive. I know, I need a good tickle, that should do the trick. *(produces tickling stick/feather duster from bag. Starts to tickle herself and laughs)* More, more. Quick help me. *(produces more feather dusters from bag, pulls off shoes, sits on edge of stage)* Help me children. Help me. *(gives dusters to about five children who come to help, laughs more, indicating under the arms as well as feet etc.,)* Oh enough. Stop. Please stop. Thank you. I think I want to live after all. Here you are. Thank you. *(exchanges Cadbury's Cream Eggs for dusters which go back in bag, sits up exhausted)* That's much better. Good exercise that. Saved myself £3. 50 for a workout down at *(local sports centre)* I don't really want to kill myself. I'm much too happy being alive. Anyway, I think Rainbow is too young for me, and I quite liked those men in the meadow, the Tollkeeper, or Rainmaker, or Gardener. Mmm, yes, which one? They all looked the same to me, didn't they to you? I wonder if they're triplets.

As she thinks, two 'Supermarket Helpers' enter through curtains with trolley, look at Dame, pick her up, dump her in trolley and start to wheel her off. Dame looks aghast at one then the other as they say

Helper 1 Looks a bit past her 'sell by' date.
Helper 2 What shall we do with her?
Helper 1 Clearance Specials?
Helper 2 Who'd want her? She'd be there for weeks.
Helper 1 Or even months.
Helper 2 Well as long as she's nowhere near the drinks counter.

As they are exiting, the Tollkeeper runs and skips in from the audience, turning around as he does so, waving his ticket

Tollkeeper *(all excited)* I've won! I've won! Yippeeeeee. I've won! *(sings, 'Have a drink , have a drink, have a drink on me. Everybody have a drink on me)* I've won etc.,

Laughalot *(jumping/scrambling out of trolley, almost turning it over, as Tollkeeper arrives on stage, and approaching him coyly)* Oh hello, my little coochie coo. *(tickles him under the chin, and making up to him)*

Tollkeeper I've won, and nobody to share my fortune with.

Laughalot *(quickly)* I'm yours.

Tollkeeper Hang on, you're the lady in the meadow, with the knicker problem. *(pause)* You owe me 2p.

Laughalot What's 2p to a man who's won the lottery? *(making up to him even more, and trying to get hold of the ticket)*

Tollkeeper Ah well, that's the question.

Laughalot *(confused)* What question?

Tollkeeper *(as per Shakespeare)* 2p or not 2p. That is the question. Whether 'tis nobler to collect, or to drop your ... (debt)

Dame lets her knickers fall before 'debt' is said. If the timing is correct, audience should shout

Audience KNICKERS!

Laughalot *(looks at audience, mouth open, then realises)* OH! Oh for one minute there I thought. *(to audience)* I know what you thought! *(hoists up knickers)* Oh, you are awful, but I like you. *(digs him in ribs)*

Tollkeeper How's about a drink, fair maid?

Laughalot You betcha! *(making up hair etc.,)* Where shall we go?

Song No 18

Music starts. Tollkeeper sings first two lines, then Dame joins in, 'Come, Come, Come And Drink Ale With Me'. Suggest only a couple of verses, ending in 'Bush, Bush'. If the audience joins in continue a little longer

Tollkeeper *(as music fades and they start to exit)* Wonder what the inside of a pub looks like?

Laughalot Don't know. Never been in one. *(fingers crossed for audience to see)* Wonder if old *(local pub person/friend)* will be there? I hear from Lottery that he's on the razzle again. Anyway, what's your name, dearie?

Tollkeeper Jack, Jack Pot!

Both exit laughing, arm in arm

Scene 3

The Palace grounds, at evening. Enter Prince and Rainbow. Courtiers are around, with Rudolph, Smelly and Trumper. Prudence enters and goes to front of stage on one side and curls up asleep, waking up at times, reacting to being stroked, as appropriate

Rainbow Sire, have you discovered the secret?

Prince Not yet Rainbow, for the crystals appear to have no magic.

Rainbow Well, something must be done. We cannot build fires to stop the Ice Queen, there is no fuel left, and the forest logs are too cold to burn.

Prince I know and ... What have you there?

Rainbow *(producing hand puppet)* It's a young Mibbie Mibbie Your Highness. I found it lost in the Black Forest. I hope you don't mind. He hasn't 'nipped' or 'bitten' me once. He's really quite sweet. *(strokes it)*

Prince looks at it cautiously

I don't think he knows how to nip or bite, in fact, he's quite a friendly little thing.

Prince strokes it

What news from Lottery?

Prince He hasn't returned yet. I don't think he is quite as 'fleet of foot' as he used to be, still, he should be back soon. I sent him as soon as we heard that the villagers had been driven from their homes, by the snowstorms.

Man in Moon I have been watching him Your Highness, he tries to serve you well, but he has stopped to help some villagers who were trapped in a snowdrift. The Ice Queen started earlier than expected, and the villagers were slow to get away.

Rainbow That wicked Ice Queen must be destroyed, or we will be!

Prince Help me now Man in the Moon. I have thought hard of the frozen lands, the turbulent seas and of my childhood. I have begun to realize what you are saying, but have not yet worked out the importance of the crystals.

Man in Moon Good my young friend. You have done well so far. Now make ready your people for the attack. All will be revealed soon, I promise.

Enter Lottery with a few villagers, all worse for wear. Smelly and Trumper sniffing around them and being patted

Prince Ah, Lottery. Good news first.

Lottery   It is a very sad, sad day today.
                 For no good news I have to say.

Prince Well, we'd better have the bad news.

Lottery   The sunny meadows are now lands of snow.
                 And drifts so high as north winds blow.
                 The Murky Marshlands exist no more.
                 Just a landscape of ice, I saw.

Prince Carry on my good friend.

Lottery   The Frosties and Mibbie Mibbies have driven villagers here.
                 It's the cold, nips and bites that they do so fear.
                 They believe you will not let them, or your kingdom fall.
                 But destroy that wicked Ice Queen, once and for all.

Villager 1 Yes, destroy the Ice Queen. Kill her.

Villager 2 And that Jack Frost, he's nearly as bad.

Villager 3 Destroy the Mibbie Mibbies too.

Villager 4 Destroy them all!

Angry villagers, shout and wave. Rainbow hides baby Mibbie Mibbie from the onslaught

Rainbow *(to audience)* Bloodthirsty lot aren't they?
Man in Moon The first snowstorm approaches Your Highness.
Laughalot *(running in)* What's happening?
Prince The Ice Queen's attack is about start.

A small spray of snow starts at one side, where the golden pot has been placed, and a couple of Frosties 'spray' a little ice

Laughalot Oh no. Must get my Hottie Bottie. *(as rushing off, knickers fall down, chased by Smelly, laughing 'barks')*
Audience KNICKERS!
Laughalot *(to audience)* Whoops. *(starts to hoist up, stops, takes them off)* I'll get my thermals. 'Winter Draws' on. *(laughs as going off, throws knickers down, goes wrong way towards snow, trips, knocks over golden pot)* whoops again. Sorry. *(twirls around and rushes out the other side)*

Prince goes to pick up the pot, and notices that the snow is melting, caused by the white crystals. He puts the spilt crystals back in the pot, then puts his finger to his mouth, as if thinking. Takes his finger away, and licks his lips, as if tasting. Looks at his finger, then tastes his finger, and looks at the white crystals in the pot - REALIZATION!

Man in Moon Your Highness, I believe you have discovered the secret.
Prince Indeed I have Man in the Moon. You have saved us all. Without this pot of 'Gold' from the end of the rainbow, the Ice Queen could have taken my Kingdom, and frozen us all.

All gather round the Prince in awe

Rainbow But Sire, it's not a pot of gold. It's a gold pot full of white crystals.
Prince *(excited)* Oh no Rainbow, this is worth more than gold. These crystals are SALT. They melt the snow and ice. It will save us all.

Song No 19

Prince sings, joined by others after the first verse, 'I Can See Clearly Now The Snow (rain) Has Gone'. As music fades

Rainbow I do not really understand Your Highness.
Villager 5 Neither do I, but we are saved. The Prince has saved us.
Prince No, it is the Man in the Moon who has saved us. It was his magic that stopped time, and let us reach the end of the rainbow, to get the secret. This golden pot of salt. With this we can stop the Ice Queen.

Rainbow But Sire, 'tis only a handful.

Prince Yes Rainbow, but the seas are full of salt, that's why they don't freeze. there is enough salt in them to stop the Ice Queen forever.

Rainbow Sire, you say 'stop', we must destroy her.

Prince No Rainbow, for wicked as she is, I will not destroy her, should I Man in the Moon?

Man in Moon Indeed not Prince Lionheart, you have learnt well, but more snow is coming. I believe it to be the main attack.

Laughalot *(rushing on)* What's happening?

Prince The Ice Queen' main attack begins.

Laughalot Oh dear. I need a drink. Where's my sherry bottle? *(rushes off)*

Rainbow Look Sire, to the north. *(points out into audience)*

Note: The whole attack is through the audience. This gives a very realistic effect, and is much enjoyment for the audience and juveniles. Spotlights on for the attack which should be done quite quickly to minimise disturbance. Ice Queen using her discretion re pace of progress. To start, gentle music comes up, and Snowflake and a few of her snowflakes enter flittering towards the stage, with Prince and others to front of stage, looking out

Prince Snowflake, come here quickly, by my side.

Snowflake goes to the Prince, and the snowflakes flutter down at the sides. The Mibbie Mibbies enter, pretending to 'nip' as they pass through the audience. These are followed by Jack Frost, Icicle and some Frosties, who hiss as they pass through. Then the Ice Queen, to menacing music, enters, commanding her forces from the centre isle, striding slowly, with three Frosties to guard her. Villagers start to cower towards back of stage, as do the other characters to a degree. Rudolph starts to fight the attackers off, but not too ferociously. The Prince stands defiant at the front

Ice Queen Move up. Attack. Take the Palace. Forward you Mibbie Mibbies. Onward Frosties. Freeze the fools etc., That's it my 'Nippies and Coldies', to the Palace. Jack, more troops, and bring the North Winds on.

Jack uses phone to try to call up the North Winds, but it doesn't work. He bashes it etc., On reaching the stage, all to sides except main characters. Mibbie Mibbies make to nip villagers, who fight them off with staves. Smelly and Trumper bark at them. Prince scatters 'salt' at the Frosties who back off to sides. Ice Queen ends up facing the Prince at the front

Ice Queen You fool. You seek to defy me. ME, the ICE QUEEN? Jack, Jack, where are the North Winds?

Jack bashes the mobile phone again

Ice Queen Oh, you and that useless contraption!

Jack Frost I told you it doesn't work in bad weather conditions.

Prince *(laughing)* You have beaten yourself. Your attack is stopped, and you cannot win.

Ice Queen Snowflake, so this is your Prince. COME HERE CHILD!

Snowflake No Mother. This where I belong. We love each other.

Ice Queen HERE. *(indicates to Frosties and Mibbie Mibbies)* ATTACK! ATTACK! Chill their bones to the marrow.

Prince They dare not, for they will be destroyed. They fear for their lives, as you should.

Ice Queen *(defiantly)* WHAT! I FEAR NO-ONE!

Rudolph comes up and 'butts' her a bit, and Mooos. Ice Queen reacts

Prince Even if you win today, some of us will escape to the Southlands. We have the secret of how to destroy you, these crystals can melt away your very existence. In the Southlands we can get more crystals from the seas, and beat you back to the Northlands where you belong. As for the Mibbie Mibbies, they are not really aggressive, they just fear your power.

Ice Queen *(listening and hesitating)* What are these 'magic crystals' that you speak of?

Prince It is SALT. Have you never wondered why you could not freeze the seas? They are full of salt. Your menacing rule is over.

Laughalot *(entering with sherry and pill bottles)* What's happening?

Rainbow WE'VE WON!

Laughalot Oh dear, I'm glad I brought my pills. *(goes to take one with a sip of sherry, then stops)* We've what?

Rainbow WE'VE WON!

Laughalot We've won. We've won. *(starts dancing round 'whooping' and hitching up her knickers)*

Smelly comes over, barks and turns around as well. They dance a little jig

Rainbow What do you mean WE. It was the Prince who saved us.

Laughalot Well I helped didn't I? I was in the thick of the battle, fought the Ice Queen I did. Beat her up and smashed ... *(arrive face to face with Ice Queen. Backs away, very frightened)* Oo err. It's her. What are we going to do with her?

Villager 3 Kill her.

Villager 4 Yes, destroy her now, and that Jack Frost.

Villager 5 And all her followers. So we can live in peace.

Villagers Down with the Ice Queen/kill her etc., *(shake fists)*

Snowflake and Icicle cling to each other in fear of the villagers. Icicle looks pleadingly at the Prince

Prince Do not worry Snowflake. I will not harm your mother.

Man in Moon You have truly learnt well Prince Lionheart. Explain to your friends, else they destroy you.

Soft music comes up

Prince *(to all)* As the Man in the Moon said, 'think on my childhood', think on yours. Look back when you were young. Did you not express delight when you saw the snowflakes falling? Did you not go out and make snowballs to throw at each other in fun? Did you not build wonderful snowmen? And the ice, was it not fun to slide on the frozen puddles, and on the ice and snow together, make the longest slide you could? Were these not happy times, filled with laughter? Well?

All 'friendly forces' are smiling and nodding as the Prince speaks

Villagers Yes Sire/Oh what fun we had etc.,
Prince Would you have me destroy all that, and not let your children have those happy times?
Villager 1 We hadn't looked at it like that Sire.
Villager 2 What are we to do then?
Man in Moon Prince Lionheart, you have discovered wisdom indeed. Your goodness will prevail over the wickedness of the Ice Queen.
Prince *(to Ice Queen)* I shall banish you to the Northlands where you can rule at will, but, you will come once a year around Christmas time, to bring happiness to all the children.

Ice Queen cringes

And to see your daughter Snowflake, whom I intend to marry.
Ice Queen WHAT - never! Snowflake is to marry Jack.
Snowflake No mother, we *(moving closer to Prince)* love each other, and anyway, Jack loves Icicle.
Icicle Oh goodie, Jackio baby. How's about a smouchie smoo?

Jack goes to Icicle and hugs/kisses her

Prince I promise not to destroy you in your ice lands, and YOU must promise not to overstay your welcome, like all good Mothers-in-law. *(to audience)* Promises must be kept, mustn't they?
Audience Yes!
Ice Queen *(crossly)* Well yes, but we'll see.
Rainbow What about the Mibbie Mibbies Sire? *(holds up the little one and strokes it, as Smelly and Trumper jump up a little to see)*
Prince The Mibbie Mibbies will return to the forest where they belong.
Rainbow Ah, I quite like mine, and he likes me. Does he have to go?
Prince That is up to him and the older Mibbie Mibbies. They can all stay if they wish, but they will have to behave themselves.

Mibbie Mibbies nod and smile

Note; please see addendum for alternative section here

Man in Moon All appears to be well Your Highness. It is time to start my night journey across the heavens. *(recites)*

I am happy now that all is well. 'Tis time to cast my romantic spell.

Scatters handful of 'golden glitter' over ensemble. Soft music comes up. Prince and Snowflake gaze at each other, as do Jack Frost and Icicle. Smelly and Trumper 'woof' at each other and snuggle up. Two girl villagers close in on Rainbow and Lottery. Dame looks around. Ice Queen stands to one side, huffing

Laughalot Where's that Potty Jack?

Jack Pot comes over to Dame. They gaze at each other as soft romantic music starts, then abruptly changes tempo to

Song No 20

'I'm Gonna Marry You' to music of 'I Wanna Be Like You' or alternative music (sheet music available). Prince (deep voice) sings first verse, all sing the chorus. Dame sings second verse, all sing chorus again. Jack Frost sings third verse, with all joining in on the final resounding chorus. Some Mibbie Mibbies and Frosties come to front of stage with Smelly, Trumper and Rudolph. All actions are as chimpanzees, knees apart with side kicks, fists clenched down towards the floor. Side steps to left and right if space permits. Other movements as thought fit, and pointing as appropriate

1. Well I'm the Prince of the Kingdom,
    And I fell in love with you.
    I don't care what your mother says.
    I'm going to marry you!
    Ohh, ooo, beee, doo. Dobee, dobee, dobee dooooo.
    He's in love with you, and he's gonna marry youu, oouu.

2. Now I'm the Dame, his Nanny,
    And I fell in love with you.
    If you win any more on the Lottery,
    Then you'll give it to me, won't you?
    Ohh, ooo, beee, doo. Dobee, dobee, dobee, dooooo.
    She's in love with you, and she's gonna marry youu, oouu.

3. Now I'm Jack Frost of the Frosties,
    And I fell in love with you.
    I don't care if you're cold outside,
    I'll warm you through and through!
    Ohh, ooo, beee, doo. Dobee, dobee, dobee, dooooo.
    He's (I'm) in love with you, and he's (I'm) gonna marry youu.
    Oh, they're (I'm) in love with you,
    And they're (I'm) gonna marrrrry Youuuuuuuuuu.

Music fades, Prince down on one knee

Prince *(to Ice Queen)* Hr, Hm Mother. May I?
Ice Queen *(grudgingly)* Oh, very well then. If you must!
Prince Princess Snowflake, will you marry me?
Snowflake *(pulling him up and hugging him)* Yes, yes.
All Hooray! Hooray!
Rainbow Wonderful - a Royal Wedding.
All Hooray! Hooray!
Laughalot Hey Jack. You want to marry me?
Jack Pot You only want me for my money, don't you?
Laughalot *(sings)* Oh no Jack, no Jack, no Jack, no. And I won't need these any
  more. *(brings out Hottie Bottie and pills, throws them away, begins hitching
  up knickers)* You to keep me warm, and no headaches! Ha!

*Meanwhile Smelly has found the Dame's knickers, discarded earlier, and has
been playing with them. He now approaches Ice Queen with them between his
teeth, as everyone watches*

Laughalot *(indicating Ice Queen)* I think he's trying to say something to you.
  (knickers fall down)
Audience KNICKERS!

Everyone gasps/giggles, except Ice Queen who haughtily 'huffs and puffs'

Laughalot What! *(to audience)* Oh, you meant her. Oh, you didn't mean her. I
  thought you did. Well thank you. Oh I see, you think I should throw these
  away *(hoists up knickers)* as well as my Hottie and pills. You were being rude
  then, weren't you? Naughty, naughty. No cheap thrills here you know. *(wags
  finger at audience)* I'm not throwing these away. *(looks at Jack, smiling)* Yet!
  (completes hoisting up knickers)
Lottery *(to Rainbow, calling over two villager girls)*
       These are two girls I saved from the snow.
       Beaut - iful eyes and cheeks that gl - ow.
       They said they would thank me as much as they can.
       Have you any ideas, you magical man?
Rainbow *(eyes girls)* Quite a few, Lottery. Quite a few. ABRACADABULOUS
  *(swirls cape, produces a long cane, takes one of the girls by the hand to front
  of stage, as music starts, stands to side of her holding the cane to the floor
  with one hand, gesturing to the moon with the other. Then, dancing to her
  other side and gesturing to her. Picks her up in his arms)* Give me the moon -
  light, give me the ga - al. And leave the rest to meeeeee. *(picks her up on 'rest',
  looks closely into her eyes on 'to', and then, jokingly, runs off with her to
  'meeeee'. But stops before offstage, puts her down on other side of the stage
  from Lottery and his girlfriend)*

Laughter and applause from those on stage

Jack Frost Pure magic Rainbow. Hey Icicle, cutie babe, will you marry me?

Icicle Sure thing Jackio. My icy go- ose pimples are already thawing.

Jack Frost We can honeymoon on the Ski Slopes you know. One of those 'freebie' holidays that Fergie *(Royal Family)* is always talking about.

Icicle No way, Jackio. Let's zap to Teneriff. We can me - lt the nights away, and, *(laughing)* make lots and lots and lots of Frosticles.

Laughalot We don't wish to know that. Kindly leave the stage!

Jack Pot Where shall we go for our honeymoon?

Laughalot How about Felixstowe?

Jack Pot Where's Felixstowe?

Laughalot On the end of Felix's foot! *(laughs outrageously, digs him in ribs, sends him flying, then composes herself)* Isn't it wonderful? All these weddings. Look, it's becoming an epidemic. *(points to Smelly and Trumper who are 'woofing' and nuzzling up to each other)* I'd be so happy if it wasn't for her. *(indicates Ice Queen)* What do we do about this old frump?

Lottery   Any punishment for her would seem a bit feeble.
            But we could marry her off - to Jeremy Beadle!

Prince Hr, hm, perhaps. anyway, will you stay for the wedding - Mother?

Snowflake Oh do mother, please.

Ice Queen *(reluctantly, but pleasantly)* If I must. But I will not stay long. I want to get back to my own cold home. Have a nice 'iced' tea, with coconut snowballs, iced buns, ice cream, and ...

Rainbow *(interrupting)* Ha, you appear to have something in common with Nanny.

Dame and Ice Queen 'humph' at each other. Ice Queen 'huffs' to one side of stage

Anyway, time to prepare for the Royal Wedding, no, lots of weddings.

All Yes/yes/happy couple/ couples/etc.,

Man in Moon This is indeed a good time Your Highness. Now that you are free from the threat of snow and ice, of a frozen landscape, the time is right for you and your Princess to build a new kingdom, a new land, a land of warmth, love and happiness. Oh, I'm so happy. *(laughs)* I'm over myself. I'm Over the Moon!

Song No 21

Whole ensemble sing, 'Over The Moon Of Love'. all sing chorus verses, including the last. The couples only (front of stage, Lottery and girl, Dame and Jack Pot, Prince and Snowflake, Jack Frost and Icicle, Rainbow and girl) sing verses 2 and 4. The last verse should build up to a crescendo, and end quite abruptly. As each word of the last line is sung, perhaps a spin by each of the girls, starting from the outside (alternating sides) of the five. Snowflake last on the beginning of the long 'Loveeee', or all together. Or all the girls, a sweeping curtsey, with gents leaning back, with arms outstretched, one hand raised to the air, the other hand holding the girl's hand. This can make a dramatic finish to the performance

1. We're over the moon, over the moon,
        Over the moon of love.
    Over the moon, over the moon,
        Over the moon of love.
2. How happy we'll be, just you and me,
        Over the moon of love,
    Your hands in mine, oh so divine,
        Over the moon of love.
3. Over the moon, over the moon,
        Over the moon of love,
    Over the moon, over the moon,
        Over the moon of love.
4. Your eyes so bright, shining at night,
        Over the moon of love,
    We'll be together, love lasts forever,
        Over the moon of love.
5. We're over the moon, over the moon,
        Over the moon of love,
    Love lasts forever, when you're together,
        Over the moon, over the moon,
        Over - the moon - of looooove.

Curtain. After the curtains have closed, in preparation for the Royal Wedding, Rainbow and Lottery come through the curtains with their two girlfriends

Rainbow Hi everyone.
Audience Hi Rainbow!

Then follows the usual 'singalong' routine. House lights up. Start with everyone being happy. Prince met his Snowflake - a Princess, wonderful etc., and suggest sing one verse only to start, with appropriate actions

Song No 22

To the tune of, 'She'll Be Coming Round The Mountains When She Comes'

1. If you're happy happy happy, clap your hands
    If you're happy happy happy, clap your hands
    If you're happy happy happy, happy happy happy
    Happy happy happy, clap your hands.

2. For, 'clap your hands' sing instead, 'stamp your feet'

Develop as desired. One side clapping, one side stamping. Then reverse sides etc., The lucky seven who guessed the rainbow colours are called on stage (collect rainbow cards). Also 'birthday' and other specials are called up, assisted by two girls, and Dame, who can enter from back of audience

Laughalot This side can clap, this side can stamp, then. alternate each time, until you get all confused, and end up stamping on your hands!

All join in for final sing-song. As frivolity ends, the 'golden pot' is brought on and given to the Dame, who hands out Cadbury's Cream Eggs to those on stage, who are then asked to return to their seats

All Well done/super/you were marvellous/ can you come back next week?

Girls wave and exit, followed by Dame who waves and lovingly says

Laughalot See you all later. Off to the Royal Wedding now. By,eee.
Rainbow I love weddings. I get ever so excited.
Lottery And do you know what - YOU are all invited. *(both wave and exit)*

Scene 3a

The Palace grounds are now decorated with flags, bunting, streamers, balloons etc., All players enter from the audience, down centre, and take their places on stage after their acknowledgement from audience

Suggested order:

> **Adult chorus** in grand costumes (back of stage)
> **Juveniles** in mix of costumes (sides, and sit on stage apron)
> **Dish and Spoon** (one front side of stage)
> **Rudolph** and **Prudence** (other front side of stage)
> **Smelly** and **Trumper** (sit on front stage, doggy-like)
> **Jack Frost** and **Icicle** (next to Dish and Spoon)
> **Ice Queen** escorted by 3 'guard' Frosties (next to Jack Frost and Icicle)
> **Rainbow** and **Lottery** (one each side of stage)

Their girlfriends close in on them. Rainbow takes off his hat and produces baby Mibbie Mibbie, strokes it. Then he and Lottery turn and 'present' **Man in the Moon** *who takes appropriate bow*

Man in Moon *(gestures to back of audience)* LOOK YONDER!

Jack Pot runs in, defending himself, Dame Laughalot is chasing him, hitting him with handbag

Laughalot *(shouting)* Tell me you'd won the lottery. You didn't say it was only £10 did you? I'll teach you. I'm worth more than £10 etc.,

As they reach the stage they compose themselves

Laughalot Said he'd buy me a gold necklace - 18 carats - look at it! *(shows necklace round her neck made of 18 carrots)*

They make up and take their bows. Jack moves to side, gesturing Dame to audience for her main applause

Laughalot *(announcing, to fanfare, drum roll etc.,)* Prince Lionheart and Princess Snowflake.

Dame moves aside as they arrive on stage in wedding attire. All cheer, some throw confetti/pull party poppers - A Real Wedding

Laughalot Three cheers for Prince Lionheart and Princess Snowflake. Hip hip *(three times)*
Lottery *(after cheers)* 'Tis time for Rainbow and I to go.
Rainbow We hope you have enjoyed the show.
Lottery The Prince and Princess are now wed.
Rainbow And off home you go to a nice warm bed.
Lottery My task is done, no more rhymes to say.
Rainbow And I'll keep my magic for another day.
Lottery We'll see you all please, at any time.
Rainbow Hope most of all, at our next pantomime.
Jack Pot *(moving to Dame)* She's forgiven me, so it's goodnight from me.
Laughalot And it's goodnight from him.

Prince and Princess move slightly forward with gesture to Man in the Moon. They face front

Prince   The Man in the Moon looked out of his moon.
                         Looked out of his moon and said,
Man in Moon   Goodnight to you, safe journey home.
                         Good health, good luck, and GOD BLESS.

Final curtain

PRODUCTION NOTES

Costumes

Costumes are often one of the most difficult aspects of a pantomime, and all credit must be given to those responsible, both for preparation and creation, and for efforts backstage during performance. Especially with Dame's outfits and with changes for juveniles. Whilst it is best to try to keep costume changes to a minimum, this can lead to a 'mundane' appearance, from the audience point of view, (though no doubt they will still enjoy it) and reduce the 'involvement' by the players themselves. Please bear this in mind. However, some costumes are suitable for the whole performance. Also, all main costumes can be 'enhanced' for the Royal Wedding.

All costumes should be predominantly silver/whites/blues in Act 1, Sc. 3 and yellows/oranges/reds in Act 2, Sc.1. Take this into account for continuity to the next scenes. This is catered for in storyline, when the travellers arrive at Buttercup Meadows, they have changed into the 'sunny' clothes provided by the villagers.

It is intended that Rainbow, Lottery, and the Mibbie Mibbies will appear in other pantomimes, thus you may wish to retain their costumes for future use.

Prince Lionheart. Traditional medieval Prince's costume with silver/gold buttoned coats, high boots, a wide, swashbuckling belt, and a splendid hat. For his travels a 'Royal' cape would be correct. Costume changes as appropriate and available.

Snowflake. Flowing white soft and flimsy material, with lace if possible. Loose and easy to swirl and flutter. White ballet shoes, and soft headband or scarf. If no wedding dress available, add a tiara, veil, bouquet etc., for Wedding scene.

Man in the Moon. Plain and simple. Long flowing sort of nightgown/kaftan. Colour to match mood, or same rich colour throughout. Yellow fancy slippers if he is to show these during the 'happy times' sequence.

Lottery. Jokers outfits, in plain colours suitable for the two colour change scenes, with small floppy hat hanging to one side. Matching upturned-toe boots give a good effect, colour changed by socks or cut-off tights over outside of boots.

Rainbow. As colourful as you like at all times. Using all the colours of the rainbow in one outfit for whole pantomime. Include a flamboyant, outrageous bow tie, and a large cape, almost to the ground, for swirling around, and a colourful hat, possibly a top hat suitably adapted. Not a pointed hat.

Ice Queen. Silver and whites/blacks from head to toe. The design matters little but she should always look 'commanding'. A flowing slim black train and small silver tiara would enhance the overall effect.

Dame Laughalot. Totally outrageous and 'over the top' at all times, with the usual heaving bosoms. Initially a bit 'Nannyish' and then 'over covered' on her travels, but completely whimsical and colourful at Buttercup Meadows. She should wear grand wigs, stylish hats/bonnets. Adorned most grandly in the Wedding Scene. With respect to her knickers falling down, they must be loose, and a bright, easily noticed, colour. A stiff wide band, perhaps cardboard, can be stitched/stapled inside at the top, so that Dame can 'push them down', instead of hitching them up. Several costume changes required.

Jack Frost. All in silver, quite simple. Suggest a bit 'snazzy' as he is a bit of a 'Jack the lad' character. Shoulder pads, large belt, and 'pixie' style silver boots.

Icicle. Silver again, if possible with a sheen to give a watery effect. Fashion heels, colourful 'shades' and appropriate coloured beads for coloured scenes. A wide coloured belt and a small bright bag containing her 'lippy', mirror, nail file etc.,

Tollkeeper/Rainmaker/Gardener/Jack Pot. A little difficult. Yellow Wellington boots throughout. Three hats; floppy 'yokel' hat as Tollkeeper, yellow rain hat as Rainmaker, woolly hat as Gardener. As each hat comes off the next is revealed. A long flowing cape, with arms holes, as Tollkeeper, and underneath this a yellow sou'wester, not fully buttoned up, leggings in matching yellow, with velcro at the back for easy removal. As Gardener, old trousers, with braces, short-sleeved sweater, shirt sleeves rolled up. As Jack Pot, back to Tollkeeper outfit.

Rudolph. As suggested, a one person cow keeps it fairly simple, but the standard two person cow creates a good effect. Ensure there are; horns, big red nose, tail and udders if possible.

Smelly and Trumper. Doggy outfits. Smelly is a bit of a rascal, a mongrel perhaps. Trumper, though sometimes a bit rough, is very ladylike. Smart coat and bonnet for her for the Wedding?

Prudence. Normal cat costume. A fluffy cat is best. Failing this a slinky feline 'body and tights' costume with long whiskers and big eyes/eye lashes.

Dish and Spoon. Can be two characters or one, but keep as simple as possible.

Chorus/Juveniles. Adults play courtiers and villagers, juveniles play courtiers and villagers' children, but are mainly; Frosties, Snowflakes, Mibbie Mibbies, Sunrays, with Raindrops and Rainbow Colours optional.

Courtiers and Villagers. Although the pantomime reflects a medieval period, courtiers can be grand and elegant, but not too lavish. Villagers wear long skirts with loose tops, or smocks and baggy trousers (string or buckle belts). Scarves, floppy hats worn by some. They should appear to be coming from a poor village.

Mibbie Mibbies. All green/green brown forest imps, preferably cuddly/furry characters, despite their apparent aggressiveness. All-in-one costumes are best.

The real distinguishing feature of the Mibbie Mibbies should be the head, similar to a small dragon, with large black eyes, and large rounded sticking up ears coming to a point at the top. Feet and hands with three pronged claws/fingers. The 'baby' Mibbie Mibbie, adopted by Rainbow, made along similar lines, either as a whole, or as a glove puppet.

Frosties. All in silver/whites. Very plain costumes. Snowflakes. All in white. Sunrays. All in yellow. Raindrops. All in white, but covered in a clear plastic to create a watery look. All-in-one poncho style sheets (shaped?) will do, or more elaborate, e.g. lace on the Snowflakes, silver belts/boots for the Frosties etc.,

Rainbow Colours. See Stage Notes if a 'made' rainbow is to be used, perhaps recommended for smaller/medium sized productions. This eliminates the need for rainbow coloured costumes, the simple approach, yet still giving an attractive impact. For multi-coloured costumes - see Stage Notes. If seven juveniles are used, (to form a half rainbow) then each should wear a colour of the rainbow: red, orange, yellow, green, blue, indigo, violet. Again, all-in-one poncho sheets will do, with additionally, a hood of same colour, with cut out eye holes, and velcro sleevelets that include the hands. If fourteen juveniles are used, the same costumes apply, and they meet up to join and make a full rainbow.

Lighting, Sound and Prop notes

As a general rule, try to 'keep it simple, it works'. This may be easier said than done in pantomime, but if we attempt to adhere to the principal, we should make progress. Much will depend upon the facilities of your theatre, and the ingenuity of the Stage Manager.

Lighting. Basic requirement is, of course, lights, some on a dimmer switch if possible. Everything after this is a bonus! A few main points where lighting changes are necessary to create an effect are:

Lights up, spotlights or House Lights; pages; 4, 5, 7, 19, 22, 40, 44, 51, 57
Lights up higher, page; 19
Blue/silver light, page; 22
Ultra Violet lighting, pages; 22, 40
Bright orange/yellow glow lighting, page; 29
Yellow/orange hues, page; 31
Strobe lighting (important see *note below)/flashing lights, page; 40
Pyrotechnics, page; 40

*Note. If Strobe lighting is used, the usual audience warning must be posted.

Sound. There are no special sound requirements, except for musical influences. The only places where crashes are needed is;

When, 'Time Stands Still'	Page 40
Rainbow smashes his '2p' on Tollkeeper's head	Page 32
Dame falls in a heap trying to jump over the moon	Page 44

These crashes can be accomplished by cymbals/pyrotechnics or even by the banging of saucepan/dustbin lids. The addition of fog/mist when time stands still will also create a good effect. Other sound effects can, of course be added as thought appropriate.

Props. This is a guideline only, and it is suggested that a full check is undertaken when properties have been finalised. The 'Props Team' are very important, and it can be fun collecting/making/arranging the props. Something will invariably go wrong, deliberately or otherwise, but the task should not be underestimated.

ACT 1, Scene 1. Duvet, yellow/white sheet. Wobbly wand for Rainbow (required throughout). Rainbow colour cards. Trick (silk scarf to bunch of flowers). Joke naked chicken. Spray cans of Christmas silver/frost. Mobile phone. Mug. Mint sweets (including 'Foxes Glacier', if possible). Hot water bottle. Large 'frost' spray. Old blow torch. Falling star (if not juvenile). Old lamp on pole. Three small packs. Dame's bag, containing; Hot water bottle, sherry bottle and pill bottle. Blanket.
Scene 2. Half a full moon. Old lamp on pole. Sticks for fire. Red cycle lamp/torch. Three small packs. Dame's bag. Blanket.
Scene 3. Duvet, silver sheet. Dame's bag. Tray with four pots and four chunks of bread. Snow and ice/frost sprays. Some straw. Bowl and spoon. Half a 'Sun', and/or bright light. Three different packs. Food bags.
Interval. (Saturdays only) Piece of paper with winning lottery numbers on.

ACT 2, Scene 1. Duvet, yellow/white sheet. Buttercups/flowers. Large fake 2p. Picnic box and other food bags containing jelly on plate and chocolate gateau. String of sausages. Dame's bag. Blanket. Tollkeeper pouch. Fake medium sized 2p on string. Fake hand. Supermarket trolley. Large pair of scissors. Wig. Lottery tickets. Large finger on a pole. Small watering can with a little water. Watch. Spade. Golden Pot with white crystals. Small fiddle. Old Large coin. Cadbury's cream Easter egg. Walkman. Small squeezy with little water. Bone. Large daisy.
Scene 2. Large daisy. Bag with; Dame's hottie bottie, pill bottle, empty sherry bottle, six feather dusters, and Cadbury's Cream Easter eggs. Supermarket trolley. Lottery ticket.
Scene 3. Duvet, yellow sheet. Baby Mibbie Mibbie. Spray snow/ice. Golden pot with crystals. Hot water bottle. Staves. Mobile phone. Sherry bottle. Pill bottle. Golden glitter. Dancing cane.
Singalong. Golden pot containing Cadbury cream Easter eggs.
Royal wedding. Duvet, silver or gold sheet. Confetti. Party poppers. Flags. Bunting. Streamers. 18 carrot necklace. Handbag. Baby Mibbie Mibbie. Use of glitter, confetti etc., may create extra clearing up, but is well worth while for effect. Perhaps you can set up a rota for clearing up after each performance.

A local supermarket will often supply a trolley, store outfits for Act 2, Sc 2, sweets/Easter Eggs etc., in return for a free advert/thank you in your programme. Add the usual supply of signs to wave from the wings 'BOO' ' BEHIND YOU' 'HISS' etc.,

Stage

No stage furniture, except the stile, is needed. Description of each scene is given at the beginning of that scene. Time has been allowed between each main scene change, with a mini-routine in front of tabs, to allow ample time for these changes.

Man in the Moon. The whole pantomime revolves around the Man in the Moon, and this major aspect should be considered before any construction commences.

The simplest approach is to paint on a moon, and have the voice speaking behind it. Alternatives to this theme are many. For example, cut a round hole in the appropriate flat/tab/screen so that the costumed player can be seen/silhouetted with lights etc.,

However, the best option is to have the Man in the Moon on some kind of platform (as in the musical 'Cats'). The following suggestions for stage construction are therefore all based upon the platform principle, bearing in mind that the two main scenes are the Palace Grounds and Buttercup Meadow, and the two minor scenes, the Black Forest Pathway and the Village at Murky Marshlands.

Smaller productions. Schools etc., A very simple concept can be used. Two sets of reversible screens, preferably on castors, painted to depict the appropriate scenes. Palace and Meadows on one set, Forest Pathway and Village on the other set. The screens not in use moved offstage, or stored behind the set in use.

The Man in the Moon, again quite simple with two options;

A. A large moon is made and placed behind the back screen, with the player sitting on a step-ladder in front of his moon to act out his part.
B. A firm bench/platform is placed on stage, (between one and two metres high) large enough for him to sit, curl up asleep, with the round moon attached at the back. Cover the bench with a duvet/sheet. The sheet could be cut leaving large pointed moonbeams that fall towards the floor. Bench can be 'disguised' with appropriate scenery, Palace turret/bush or bank in the meadow/village wall etc., The platform has a very useful purpose in Act 2, Sc 1 when the treasures at the end of the rainbow can be concealed there.

Medium sizes productions. Medium sized halls, small theatres etc., It is likely, with a larger stage, that you will have the additional facilities of some, or all of, a rear set of flats, a backcloth, frontcloth, Stage Curtains and one or two side flats. Side flats can be dealt with as above, but, if not reversible, it may be best to have the 'Night Sky/Moon' permanently on the front flats. The rear side flats need to depict three scenes; Palace Meadows, Village scene and Buttercup Meadows. The best way to deal with these is for one scene to be painted on the flat, and loose covers (cloth or stiff paper) that depict the other scenes, made for easy attachment over the flat, by hooks, nails etc., at the top. Frontcloth should depict the 'Black Forest Pathway'. Backcloth the 'Village at Murky Marshlands'.

If your theatre has a trap door, this is ideal for the Rainbow's Treasures.

With reference to the 'Cow jumping over the Moon' routine, this is basically a farcical business and it matters not too much that the cow doesn't actually go over the moon. If you have a rope and pulley of course use it to maximum effect. If you have a sturdy beam/scaffold, try a few 'jumps' at rehearsals, pulling off or on - make it part of the routine!

Man in the Moon can have a strong structure (pallet-size mini-tower system?) fixed to rear flat supports or the wall. Two, to two and a half metres, is probably about right. Alternatively you may decide to hang or brace the platform from the top of the Stage Structure.

Tree flaps Act 1, Sc 2 optional. Mibbie Mibbies appear at the side of the stage, and poke their heads through flaps. These can be either cut intoside screens/flats, or cutout trees/trunks with flaps can be added to the set.

Stile. Act 2, Sc 1. This should be made as a simple one step. I suggest it is kept lower than normal to make entrance easy.

Rainbow. Act 2, Sc 1. A full rainbow of plywood/hardboard/cardboard should be made large enough for the impact it deserves. hinged if need be, as necessary, with holding handles at rear, and even complete with castors.

Dance routine. If using the full rainbow system (as opposed to the rainbow of costumes) Some Sunrays and Raindrops move off stage as 'Rainbow Colours' come on, and two of them can position themselves behind the Rainbow and slowly move onto stage. The 'Rainbow Colours' can dance around/through it, before they move off stage or sit/stand at one/both ends. Or the juveniles in multi-coloured costumes can dance around the 'made rainbow'. Or you could have no rainbow costumes at all, but have more Sunrays and Raindrops dancing around/through the 'made rainbow' until it is on stage, then move off.

Addendum

This addendum can replace section as indicated at top of Page 54 in the script.

Man in Moon All appears to be well Your Highness. It is time to start my night
  journey across the heavens. *(recites)*
    I am happy now that all is well. 'Tis time to cast my romantic spell.

*Scatters handful of 'Golden Glitter' over ensemble (soft music up). Prince and
Snowflake gaze at each other, as do Jack Frost and Icicle. Smelly and Trumper
'woof' at each other and snuggle up. Two girl villagers close in on Rainbow and
Lottery. Dame looks around, and Ice Queen stands to one side, huffing*

Laughalot Where's that Potty Jack?

Jack Pot comes to Dame. They gaze at each other

Song No 20

'My Friend The Moon Man', sung to tune of 'My Friend The Witch Doctor'. Prince (deep voice) sings first verse, and all sing chorus. Dame sings second verse, and all sing chorus again. Icicle sings third verse, and all join in resounding last chorus. Some juveniles can come to front of stage, with Smelly, Trumper and Rudolph. Actions; toe/heel side movements with knees bent/hands crossing over. Also a clap/stamp after each line of verse

1.   My friend the Moon Man, he told me what to do.
       My friend the Moon Man, he told me what to say.
       And then he said that you'd be mine, if I said this to you.
              Ooo, Eee, Ooo, Ahh, Ahh.
              Ting tang walla walla bang bang.
              Ooo, Eee, Ooo, Ahh, Ahh.
              Ting tang walla walla bang bang.
2.   My friend Prince Lionheart, he told me what to do.
       My friend Prince Lionheart, he told me what to say.
       He said you'd give me all your money, if I said this to you.
              (chorus repeat) Ooo, Eee, Ooo, Ahh, Ahh etc.,
3.   My friend Snowflake, she told me what to do.
       My friend Snowflake, she told me what to say.
       She said that you would warm me up, if I said this to you.
              (chorus repeat) Ooo, Eee, Ooo, Ahh, Ahh etc.,
              (add at end) Ooo, Eee, Ooo, Ahha, Ahh.
              Ting tang walla walla bang bang. Ooo, Eee, Ooo *(song slows)*
       I love you. And I'mmm gonnaaa marrrry - Youuuuu.

Music fades. Prince down on one knee

Prince *(to Ice Queen)* Hr, hm Mother. May I?
Ice Queen *(grudgingly)* Oh, very well then. If you must.
Prince Princess Snowflake, will you marry me?
Snowflake *(pulls him up and hugs him)* Yes! Yes!
All Hooray! Hooray!
Rainbow Wonderful! A Royal Wedding.
All Hooray! Hooray!
Laughalot Hey Jack. You want to marry me?
Jack Pot You only want me for my money, don't you?
Laughalot *(sings)* Oh no Jack. No Jack. No Jack. No. And I won't need these any more. *(brings out Hottie Bottie and pills, throws them away, hitches up knickers)* You to keep me warm and no headaches! Ha ha.

Smelly has found Dame's knickers, that were earlier discarded, and is playing with them. Now approaches Ice Queen with them between his teeth. Everyone looks, and Dame indicates to Ice Queen

Return to script